JESUS OF NAZARETH

JESUS
OF NAZARETH

HARRY EMERSON FOSDICK

Illustrated by Steele Savage

RANDOM HOUSE   NEW YORK

CONTENTS

1

JESUS' BOYHOOD

This book is about a man whom Thomas Jefferson called "The most sublime personality of whom history has a record." Jesus was born in a humble carpenter's home; he lived no more than thirty-three years; he had no wealth or public position to help him; his character and the truth he believed in were his only means of influencing the world. Yet today 800 million people profess to be his disciples.

Indeed, even if we are not his disciples, when we wish to tell when any event in history happened, we date it by his birth. Augustus Caesar, Emperor of Rome, was born, we say, in 63 B.C., and died in 14 A.D.; B.C. means "before Christ," and A.D. stands for the Latin words Anno Domini, meaning "in the year of the Lord." Even by our dating of historic

3

events we confess that the coming of Jesus was a turning point of history.

Jesus was born in Palestine in the village of Bethlehem, but he grew up in the village of Nazareth. Palestine is a fascinating country—all ups and downs from Mount Hermon, 9300 feet above sea level, to the Dead Sea, 1290 feet below sea level. Look at the map and imagine yourself starting on foot or donkey-back from Bethlehem and going north, past the city of Jerusalem, about three days' journey to Nazareth. From the highlands of Judaea where Jerusalem stands—2600 feet above sea level—you pass through the hilly country of Samaria and then, while you are still thirty-five miles away, you can see upon the ridge of Galilee some of the houses of Nazareth. Then after crossing the plain of Esdraelon at sea level, you climb the Galilean foothills a thousand feet above the plain and there, nestling in a sheltered valley, you find Nazareth where Jesus spent his boyhood.

In Nazareth today guides will show you many

4

places associated with Jesus. They will show you
the workshop where his father Joseph labored as a
carpenter, the kitchen where his mother Mary
cooked, and still others too. But there is no convincing reason to believe that these sites are genuine. One place in Nazareth, however, you can be
sure about; it was certainly there when Jesus was
a boy—the village spring where throughout the centuries the townsfolk have come to draw their water.
Indeed, this spring explains why the village grew
there in the first place, for Palestine is a thirsty
land whose settlements cluster around supplies of
water.

Imagine yourself standing beside that spring
nearly two thousand years ago and watching the
villagers coming to fill their earthen jars. Mary
comes, with Jesus beside her to help her carry the
heavy load. Take a good look at him! He seems like
the other boys who throng about the spring. He is,
let us say, ten or twelve years old. Who at that
time could possibly have imagined that some two

5

thousand years afterward millions of people around the world would be singing hymns like this about that boy:

> *All hail the power of Jesus' name!*
> *Let angels prostrate fall;*
> *Bring forth the royal diadem,*
> *And crown him Lord of all!*

Many marvelous stories are told about Jesus, some of them so marvelous that they are difficult for our modern minds to accept. But nothing is more amazing about him than the plain fact that after all the centuries a leading historian can say of that lad helping Mary with her water jar, "His is easily the dominant figure in history."

This book will try to tell the story of that boy.

It is often said that the four Gospels tell us practically nothing about Jesus' boyhood, but the fact is that throughout his career we catch glimpses of his life in Nazareth. Luke says: "The child grew and became strong, filled with wisdom; and the favor of

God was upon him. . . . And Jesus increased in wisdom and in stature, and in favor with God and man." That is a very brief summary of an extraordinary boy's development but we surely can fill in some details.

For one thing Joseph must have been a good father to the family for, had he been unjust and unkind, how could Jesus have grown up thinking of God as Father? To be sure, the idea that God is Father both of the nation and of the individual was in Jesus' Jewish heritage, and phrases like "O Lord, Father and God of my life" and "I will thank Thee, my God, my Father" represent good Jewish teaching. Jesus, however, lifted up this picture of God as a merciful Father until it became more important and meaningful than anyone else had ever made it. "Father" was his principal name for God. When, at the age of twelve, he explained to his parents why he had stayed in the temple, he said, "Did you not know that I must be in my Father's house?" And on the cross he cried, "Father, into Thy hands I commit my spirit." So we may be confident that Jesus grew up in a home where the word "father" meant kindness, justice and sustaining strength.

Joseph was a carpenter, making wooden handles for plows, yokes and goads for oxen, and doors for houses and sheepfolds. As Jesus grew up, he too was taught the trade. Among many peoples manual laborers have been looked down upon as inferiors, but that was not so among the Jews. They honored the laboring man. "The tradesman at his work," they said, "need not stand up in the presence of the greatest Doctor." Once, however, in later years when Jesus was attracting great crowds around him, he returned to Nazareth, and his fellow-townsmen were astonished that he knew so much, taught with such authority and wielded so wide an influence. "Is not this the carpenter," they exclaimed in surprise, "the son of Mary and brother of James and Joses and Judas and Simon, and are not his sisters here with us?"

So Jesus grew up as the oldest son in a large, hard-working family, and one proof that it was a happy household is suggested by Jesus' love of

Jesus was taught carpentry.

children. "He took them in his arms, and blessed them, laying his hands upon them"—so Mark tells us. Once, when his disciples were selfishly discussing which one of them was the greatest, Jesus, to teach them humility, "took a child and put him in the midst of them; and taking him in his arms, he

9

said to them, 'Whoever receives one such child in my name receives me.'" And once, when the boys and girls who were being brought by their parents to see Jesus were being shooed off by the impatient disciples, Jesus, we read, was "indignant" and "rebuked" them, saying: "Let the children come to me, do not hinder them; for to such belongs the kingdom of God." Such warm-hearted care for children must have started in Jesus' home in Nazareth.

Moreover, we know pretty well what kind of house Jesus lived in. In the lowlands where stone is scarce houses were made of sun-dried brick, but in villages like Nazareth, on the ridges where rock is plentiful, they were generally made of stone. Each house had one large square room. The walls of rough-dressed stone were three to four feet thick, and the roof too was often made of stone slabs, resting on rafters and covered with clay rolled hard to shed the rain. An outside stairway ran up to the roof, for that was a cool place to sleep in hot weather. It was also a convenient place for drying clothes and, as I myself have seen in Galilee, a welcome grazing ground for goats when grass thrust itself up through the clay.

Inside the house the outstanding feature was a raised platform, eight or ten feet above the ground, supported by stone arches and reached by a narrow flight of steps. Here the family slept at night. Two small windows furnished all the light and air save that which might come through the door, and an oven furnished warmth in winter and was the family's cooking place. In winter, too, beneath the family's raised platform the household animals— goats, sheep, dogs and chickens—spent the night.

This explains what probably happened at the inn in Bethlehem. Luke tells us that, when Jesus was about to be born, Joseph and Mary had to go to Bethlehem, six miles south of Jerusalem. The Roman emperor had ordered a census to be taken and Joseph, who was descended from David, went to the "city of David," which was Bethlehem, to be enrolled. When we Westerners read that "there was no place for them in the inn," and that Mary gave birth to Jesus in a manger, we naturally think that Joseph and Mary had been crowded out of the house into the barn or stable. But the story in Matthew says clearly that when the Wise Men found Jesus they went "into the house." Apparently what happened was that the whole elevated sleeping platform was full, and Mary and Joseph spent the night with the cattle on the ground. Giving birth to Jesus there, Mary "wrapped him in swaddling clothes, and laid him in a manger."

When Jesus traveled over Palestine in his later years he saw other kinds of houses—some made of mud-brick and some with thatched roofs of woven reeds—but in his boyhood in Nazareth he almost certainly lived in the kind of stone house we have described.

Jesus' boyhood in that home deeply influenced him all his life. He was indeed an extraordinary person for he kept seeing spiritual meaning in the simple, daily doings of the family. In later years he used them in sayings that for centuries mankind has read and meditated on and tried to live by. When he wanted to teach his disciples that his vital gospel could change the whole world, he recalled his mother making bread, and said that his kingdom is "like yeast, taken by a woman and put into three basins of flour until the whole lot has risen." When he wanted to persuade his disciples to stand up for him and let their light be seen, he remembered his mother lighting the family's lamp—a little earthenware bowl with olive oil and a wick in it—and putting it, not "under a bushel, but on a stand, and it gives light to all in the house." When he wanted to make his disciples trust God's goodness, he recalled Joseph's care for his family and said: "What man of you, if his son asks him for a loaf, will give him a stone? Or if he asks for a fish, will give him a serpent?"

That baked earth oven in Jesus' home—two feet high and two feet wide, in which dry grass was burned to do the cooking—would not seem impressive to us, but Jesus, teaching how some things swiftly pass away and are gone, talked about "the grass of the field, which today is alive and tomorrow is thrown into the oven." He even remembered the moths and the rust that damaged the family's clothing and utensils and he warned his followers against centering their desire merely on things "where moth and rust consume." And he drew lessons which the world still needs from watching new unshrunken patches put on old garments, and fresh grape juice poured into an old wineskin to ferment. The unshrunken patch, when washed, tore loose and ruined the old garment, he said, and the new wine burst the old wineskin. He was pleading for a real change in his people's thinking about religion, not just the patching up of old customs. One wonders if anybody in his family ever guessed what was going on in that boy's mind as, growing up, he began to see such deep meanings in such small events.

Of another thing in Jesus' boyhood we may be sure: he loved the out-of-doors. Well he might, for the scenery from the hill above Nazareth is glorious. Jesus must often have climbed that hill when he was a boy. To the southwest at least twenty miles away one sees the glint of the sun on the Mediterranean Sea. To the south lies the vast sweep of the plain of Esdraelon with the mountain ridges beyond, and to the east one looks far over the Jordan valley. Turning northward, one can see the snow-crowned crest of Mount Hermon some sixty miles away. When in later years Jesus said that a man of strong faith could say to a mountain, "Be taken up and cast into the sea," and it would obey him, I wonder if he was not thinking of the most impossible thing he could imagine—Mount Hermon being cast into the Mediterranean.

One cannot think of the out-of-doors in Galilee without thinking of the wild flowers. They are gorgeous. Jesus said of them that "Even Solomon in all his glory was not arrayed like one of these." In the springtime when the rains are over they clothe all Palestine with beauty and nowhere are they more plentiful and colorful than in Galilee. "Consider the lilies of the field, how they grow," Jesus exclaimed. We must not think of the flowers he thus admired as

The scenery from the hill above Nazareth is glorious.

being what we Americans commonly call "lilies." They are anemone, poppy, phlox, lupine, oleander —scores of varieties in such brilliance and profusion as I, for one, never saw elsewhere.

The out-of-doors for the boy Jesus, however, meant something more practical and down-to-earth than glorious scenery and flowers. Probably Joseph had a garden plot on which the family's vegetables were grown, and perhaps there were goats to supply the

family with milk. Agriculture was the major industry
in Galilee and certainly Jesus, as his later teaching
shows, knew all about sheep and shepherds, about
plowing, sowing and harvesting, about vineyards and
vine-dressers, and about trees of which he often
speaks. "Are grapes gathered from thorns, or figs
from thistles?" he says. "So every sound tree bears
good fruit." As for wild animals, Jesus talks about
foxes and wolves, scorpions and snakes, eagles and
ravens. One cannot understand Jesus without sharing
his knowledge and his love of the out-of-doors.

About the kind of education that a boy like Jesus
would receive in such a town as Nazareth we know
a good deal from many sources. The Jews were well-
educated people. One rabbi even exclaimed: "Perish
the sanctuary but let the children go to school!" Josephus, the famous Jewish historian, who was born
in Jerusalem in 37 A.D., and later was governor of
Galilee, wrote: "Above all we pride ourselves on the
education of our children." Jesus' training, of course,
began in the home but when he was six years old he

started going to school in the village synagogue. It would not seem much of a school to us. The children did not study the kind of subjects our boys and girls are taught. Certainly there were no courses in science. Seated on the floor in a semicircle they learned by heart the passages of Scripture which the teacher recited to them. They all spoke a language called Aramaic, but the sacred writings of the Jewish Torah—the Law—and of the Prophets and the Psalms were written in Hebrew. So Jesus and his fellow students must have learned at least some Hebrew, first the alphabet, then the vocabulary and the grammar, so that they could understand their Bible in its original tongue.

Probably not all the students really mastered Hebrew. In the synagogue service on the Sabbath, the rabbi first read the Scripture lesson in Hebrew and then translated it into Aramaic so that all could understand. Jesus, however, evidently did learn Hebrew. We are told of one occasion when he was asked to speak at the synagogue service in Nazareth and, handed the scroll of Isaiah which he asked for, he

18

found the passage he wanted and read it to the people, doubtless translating it into Aramaic.

Then, when he was twelve years old, came the great day when he was publicly presented to the congregation and told to read a passage from the Torah. After that he no longer came to the Sabbath service with Mary and sat as a child with the women, but as a male member of the synagogue sat with the men. Perhaps in celebration of this event, his parents took Jesus with them to Jerusalem that year for the feast of the Passover. Along with a large company of fellow pilgrims one imagines the family, including the twelve-year-old Jesus, crossing the plain of Esdraelon, going down the Jordan valley to Jericho, and then climbing the steep ascent to the Holy City.

It was a thrilling experience for Jesus. But most of all he was fascinated by the rabbis who taught the people in the temple courts. Who can guess what kind of teacher he had had in Nazareth, what questions his mind had asked, what discussions went on in the synagogue school about what should be done and not done on the Sabbath day, about what one should or should not eat? Here in Jerusalem, at any rate, Jesus could listen to the leading rabbis of his people. He was so captivated that he stayed behind when his family started for home. They went a whole day's journey before they discovered he was missing. Returning to Jerusalem, they searched for him three anxious days and then "found him in the temple sitting among the teachers, listening to them and asking them questions." And Luke adds: "All who heard him were amazed at his understanding and his answers."

They might well have been amazed. Something was going on inside that boy's mind whose consequence they could not possibly have guessed. Ideas were surging there, convictions were growing which two thousand years afterward millions would think are the only answer to the world's problems.

While Jesus' schooling probably stopped in his thirteenth year, his reading certainly did not. In later years he baffled his opponents repeatedly by apt quotations from the Scriptures. He knew his Bible—not only what we now call the Old Testament, but other books including *The Testament of the Twelve Pa-*

"All who heard him were amazed . . ."

triarchs, which scholars are sure he must have read. He was a serious, studious youth. As time went on convictions about who he was and what God wanted him to do grew strong in him until, as a man, he proclaimed a gospel that is still the inspiration of millions.

So Jesus lived in Nazareth until he was about thirty years old. Sometime during his youth it is probable that Joseph died. Joseph is never mentioned in the Gospels after that trip to Jerusalem when Jesus was twelve years old. His death must have left Jesus with a heavy responsibility for the support of his family. A powerful, driving sense of mission was growing in him; he saw ever more clearly what God wanted him to be and do; but apparently he stood by his family and took care of them until his brothers grew up and took over. Then the days came when he felt free to begin his great crusade—the most important event in the spiritual history of man.

2

JESUS' GREAT DECISION

When Jesus began his public ministry his fellow-countrymen were a disturbed and anxious people. They had been under foreign rule for many years and they hated it. When first the Roman Empire began extending its sovereignty over what we now call the Middle East the Jews had fought valiantly for their independence. One enemy after another, however, pillaged and plundered them. Then in 37 B.C. Herod the Great, a forceful chieftain from Edom, seized control of Palestine and was appointed king by the Roman senate. His siege of Jerusalem ended in a brutal massacre of the inhabitants—men, women and children. It was so bloodthirsty a slaughter that Josephus tells us "Herod's soldiers did their utmost that not a man from the other side be left alive."

Herod was a cruel king who in the course of his

25

reign slew two of his own sons and their mother, his favorite wife, because he suspected their loyalty. One historian says about him: "He stole along to his throne like a fox; he ruled like a tiger and died like a dog." To be sure, there was another side to him. He loved to erect magnificent buildings. He tried to endear himself to the Jews by rebuilding their temple in Jerusalem. In 20-19 B.C. he tore down the old temple and built a splendid new one which in Jesus' lifetime was not yet completely finished. Nevertheless, Herod was a cruel man and a stooge of the Romans, and the Jewish people despised him.

When Jesus was a child Herod died and the Roman Emperor Augustus divided the government of Palestine among Herod's sons. Galilee, where Jesus lived, was ruled by Herod Antipas, and we shall hear more about him. Judaea, where Jerusalem was, was ruled by Archelaus. He turned out to be so intolerably bad that fifty Jewish leaders went to Rome and persuaded Augustus to exile Archelaus and to rule Judaea directly through a representative called a "procurator." That explains why, when Jesus was crucified, Jerusalem was in charge of a Roman governor, Pontius Pilate.

Some Jews, of course, nestled up to the Romans and gained what they could for themselves by being friends of the ruling power. This was especially true of the Sadducees. They held all the important high priestly posts in Jerusalem and grew rich and powerful by co-operating with the Romans instead of opposing them. Josephus called them "aristocrats," and they were among those who in the end caused Jesus to be crucified, because they feared that he would stir up the people and bring down the Emperor's vengeance on them.

At the other extreme from the Sadducees were the Zealots. They were fighting fanatics who planned one rebellion after another in the hope of driving the Romans out. In Galilee especially these rebels were numerous and strong. When Jesus was a boy one hot-headed leader, named Judas, organized a revolt and tried to capture Sepphoris, the capital of Galilee, less than five miles from Nazareth. He wanted to seize the arsenal of Roman weapons stored there. A

Roman legion marched against Judas, defeated him, set Sepphoris on fire, and crucified along the roadsides hundreds of the captured insurrectionists. Jesus may well have seen the burning city from the hills above Nazareth and perhaps he saw the rebels nailed to their crosses.

Most of Jesus' fellow-countrymen, however, neither played up to Rome, like the Sadducees, nor tried violent rebellion against her, like the Zealots. The Pharisees, for example, thought that appeasing Rome was cowardly and that fighting Rome was futile. The Pharisees were the most popular Jewish party in Jesus' day. Their hope of Rome's overthrow and the victorious release of Israel lay in their expectation that God would soon send His Messiah, who would do for them what they could not do for themselves.

"Messiah" in Hebrew means the "Anointed One" and "Christ" means the same in Greek. Through the long years when the Jews were crushed by one conqueror after another the expectation that God's Messiah would soon come to deliver them had grown hot and strong. God would not much longer allow His people so to suffer, they believed. His "Anointed One" would suddenly appear and lead the Jews to glorious triumph.

When Jesus began his public ministry his people, whether in Palestine or in the far lands where they were scattered, were seething with this exciting hope. While they agreed, however, in expecting the Messiah's coming, they had many different ideas about what he would be like. Some thought he would be an extraordinary man, rising from among the people. "A man shall arise . . . like the sun of righteousness," they said. Some pictured the Messiah's coming in terms of a nationalistic Jewish victory over the Gentiles. He would "execute an everlasting vengeance on our enemies," they said. Others pictured the Messiah as a benediction to the whole world, Jews and Gentiles alike. "No war shall there be any more," they said; "there shall be peace in all the earth." Still others, far from picturing the Messiah as a man, imagined him as a divine being in the heavens, waiting to descend in glory and usher in his kingdom on the earth.

All this explains why, when Jesus was convinced

that he himself was the promised Messiah, he faced one of his most difficult problems: making clear to his disciples and to his people what kind of Messiah he proposed to be.

One day when Jesus was a young man the first rumor reached Nazareth about a rousing new preacher who, down the river Jordan not far from where it flows into the Dead Sea, was stirring great crowds with his exciting message. His name was John and he was a strange figure, unlike anyone whom we could expect to see in our modern world. He had given up all the comforts of civilized life and had retreated to the wilderness, there to think out the message which God wanted him to bring to his people. When at last he began his preaching at the fords of Jordan, the Gospels tell us that he was roughly clothed in a garment made from the hide of a camel, with a leathern belt about his waist, and that the food he ate was locusts and wild honey.

John proclaimed the speedy coming of the Messiah. "After me comes he who is mightier than I," John cried, "the thong of whose sandals I am not worthy to stoop down and untie." This announcement that the "Anointed One" was at hand was usually made to comfort and inspire the people, but John proclaimed it in a way that was not comfortable at all. If the Messiah was coming, he argued, then all the people must repent of their sins and clean up their lives so that they might worthily receive him. Personal lives cleansed of their evil and devoted to the right—*that* was the only "red carpet" the Messiah wanted rolled out for his approach.

So John thundered against the individual and social sins of his people. He attacked their stinginess. "He who has two coats, let him share with him who has none," he said, "and he who has food, let him do likewise." He told the tax gatherers to "Collect no more than is appointed you"; and to soldiers who asked him what they should do, he said: "Rob no one by violence or by false accusation, and be content with your wages." So John combined the hope of the Messiah's coming with a demand that the people should be worthy of his arrival. "Repent ye," he cried. And because he was so powerful a personality and so able a preacher, the crowds thronged to hear him, and he baptized them in the Jordan as a sign that they were to live cleansed lives.

All up and down the Jordan valley, up the Judaean hills to Jerusalem, around the Sea of Galilee, from village to village until they reached Nazareth, reports of John the Baptist's preaching spread. And one day —one of the most decisive in his life—Jesus put down his carpenter's tools, bade farewell to his family, and started for the fords of Jordan to see and hear for himself.

Who can guess what had been going on in Jesus' mind all those thirty years in Nazareth? Certainly there had been growing in him a strong conviction that God had for him a special mission to fulfil. He could not always be simply a carpenter in Nazareth —he was sure of that. Truths were growing real to him, ideas were surging in his soul. He was convinced he must proclaim these to his anxious, restless, rebel-

lious countrymen. This overwhelming sense of voca-
tion—that he was an "Anointed One," perhaps *the*
"Anointed One" called by God to save his people—
more and more possessed him.

It was not vanity or self-conceit that caused him
so to think of himself. No one supposes that vanity
and self-conceit caused Beethoven to feel the call to
create music or Michelangelo to create art. Jesus must
have struggled against the thought that he was the
Messiah, and he must humbly and sometimes fearfully
have prayed to be saved from such tremendous responsibility. But there were voices in his soul that he
could not silence. God was calling him.

Then at the Jordan—when he heard John preach,
talked with him, and at last was baptized by him—
all this hidden conviction about his mission, which
one suspects even his own family had not guessed,
burst into full flower. His baptism was the decisive
experience of his life. The Gospels tell the story in
dramatic language. When he came out of the water,
"he saw the heavens opened and the Spirit descend-

33

ing upon him like a dove; and a voice came from heaven, 'Thou art my beloved Son; with thee I am well pleased.'"

That was one of the great moments of history. From that experience Jesus went forth, sure that he was the Messiah. He would not then have used that word about himself. It was his secret. It presented a staggering problem, for he was going to be a kind of Messiah of whom his people had not dreamed.

This explains why, immediately after his baptism, Jesus went alone into the wilderness—the barren wastelands above the Jordan—and fasted for forty days while he wrestled with the question how he should use his power as God's "Anointed One." What happened during those forty days of solitude no one could have known except Jesus himself. What the Gospels tell us about those days of temptation, therefore, Jesus must first have told his disciples. He said that there were three major temptations which he had to meet and master before he began his public ministry.

Before we describe them, let us consider one matter which sometimes makes the Gospels difficult for the modern reader to understand. The Jews in general and Jesus in particular commonly used language full of pictures and similes or told stories, called parables, to express their thoughts. When Isaiah prophesied a glad day coming, he did not say simply that a prosperous era would in time arrive; he said: "The mountains and hills before you shall break forth into singing, and all the trees of the field shall clap their hands." This dramatic way of expressing ideas was part of Jesus' heritage and he used it in unforgettable pictures and parables.

If we want to say that small beginnings can have big endings, we should probably state it that way in plain language. But Jesus never would have said it so. He said that a mustard seed is the smallest of all seeds but it "becomes the greatest of all shrubs, and puts forth large branches, so that the birds of the air can make nests in its shade." If we want to tell someone that he should face up to his own faults before criticizing the faults of others, we should probably say it in just that plain way. Jesus, however, invariably put the truth into a picture: "Why do you see the speck that is in your brother's eye, but do not notice the log that is in your own eye?" We Westerners do not naturally talk that way, but if we are to understand Jesus we must face the fact that he stated his truths and described his experiences in picturesque language which must always be taken seriously but cannot always be taken literally.

This, then, is the way Jesus pictured his three great temptations. First, the tempter—imagined by the people of that time as a real person, called Satan—told him that, if he was the Son of God, he should satisfy his hunger by commanding that "These stones become bread." To understand what this temptation really meant we must remember that, in picturing the new era when the Messiah came, the Jews imagined a time of wealthy prosperity when everybody would be rich, all bodily ills would be done away with, and all would have plentiful food. Well, Jesus always cared about men's bodies; he healed their diseases, he wanted the poor fed and he attacked selfish rich men

His baptism was the decisive experience of his life.

who made living hard for the common people. The question which the tempter raised was this: should he make the physical welfare of the people the first aim of his ministry? Should he try mainly to make everyone rich and well-fed? To this he answered, No! While man must have bread, he said, "Man shall not live by bread alone, but by every word that proceeds from the mouth of God." So Jesus' mission, while it included man's material welfare, was centered in man's spiritual need.

In the story of the second temptation Satan is pictured as taking Jesus up to Jerusalem, setting him on the highest pinnacle of the temple and telling him to jump off and trust God by a miracle to save him. What this means is clear. Jesus did have extraordinary powers. He could do astonishing things, especially in healing the sick. Make this wonder-working power the center of your mission, said the tempter; get a reputation as a great magician and so win a following. To this temptation Jesus again said, No! He did not want to be thought of simply as a wonder-worker whom the people came to gaze at as though he were a show. He wanted to get at people's minds and hearts with his spiritual message. Time and time again during Jesus' ministry, when he did some marvelous thing in helping people, he told them to keep still about it and not tell anyone. One of the things he feared most was that people would seek him out mainly to see him work miracles. He wanted most of all to reach their souls with his spiritual gospel.

In the third temptation, the tempter is pictured as taking Jesus to the top of "an exceeding high mountain" from which he could see the whole world, and promising Jesus that he should reign over all of it if only he would fall down and worship Satan. This means, of course, that Jesus was tempted to do evil in the false hope that good might come of it. He was being tempted to accept the Zealots' violent methods, for example, to become a military leader, to try by Satanic means to establish God's kingdom on the earth. Once more Jesus faced the tempter with a resounding No! He would not try to serve God by bow-

39

He went into the wilderness and fasted for forty days.

ing down to Satan. His message would be not bloody violence but: "Blessed are the peacemakers for they shall be called sons of God."

So Jesus wrestled with his problems. He would not forget men's souls in caring for their bodies; he would not depend on miracles to win his people's favor; he would not use Satanic means, like violence, to gain his victory. A spiritual gospel, calling for real goodness in one's inner life and depending not on force but on heartening goodwill—*that* was his choice. But who then could have guessed what that choice was going to cost him? And who could have imagined what world-wide results of it the centuries would see?

3

JESUS BEGINS HIS
PUBLIC MINISTRY

Many boys and girls get their first impression of Jesus from the Christmas stories. The angels singing of "peace on earth, goodwill toward men," the shepherds gathered at the manger in Bethlehem, the three Wise Men following the star until they find Mary and the babe—these stories are inseparable from Christmas in the home and church, and they clothe with beauty the coming of the Christ Child. Even in the Christmas stories, however, there is a rougher note. Herod the Great, we are told, "in a furious rage" ordered the murder of all the boys in Bethlehem who were two years old or under. He wanted to get rid of the Christ Child, concerning whom the three Wise Men had told him. Not being sure just where to find the Christ Child, he killed all the young boys in Bethlehem. Jesus escaped, we read, only because Joseph and Mary fled with him to Egypt.

If we are to understand Jesus' life we cannot leave out that rougher note. He faced an unruly and often brutal generation. He was not simply a lovely character. He was a tremendous, courageous person who feared no man. That day when, hungry and haggard, he came out of the wilderness after forty days of fasting and inner struggle, he faced a situation which in the end would call for more daring courage than even soldiers need.

Almost immediately the first hard blow fell. Herod Antipas arrested John the Baptist for denouncing him and threw him into prison. Herod Antipas had broken up the marriage of his half-brother Philip, and had taken his wife. If only John the Baptist could have kept still about this evil act, he would have been safe. But John could not keep still. He was determined to call his people to a good life, and when their ruler did this wrong deed John denounced him. Herod Antipas imprisoned John and ended his ministry.

Jesus' admiration for John the Baptist was deep and

strong. "Truly, I say to you," Jesus once exclaimed, "among those born of women there has risen no one greater than John the Baptist." But now John's voice was silenced and his disciples were scattered. Thus it was when Jesus, known to only a few of his people as a carpenter from Nazareth, began his public ministry.

The results were astonishing. Jesus left the fords of Jordan and went north to the Sea of Galilee. He probably knew it well, for it is only a six-hour donkey-back ride from Nazareth. The Sea—which we would call a lake—is 685 feet below sea level. It is thirteen miles long and eight miles wide at its broadest, and in Jesus' day nine large towns lined its western shores. Josephus wrote enthusiastically about the fertile soil, the abundant fish, and the prosperous industry of the lakeside. Here in one of the busiest and most populous parts of Palestine Jesus began to gather disciples and to preach his gospel.

He had met his first disciples among the followers of John the Baptist. Simon—who was afterward called Peter—and Andrew were brothers. So too were James and John, the sons of Zebedee. Almost certainly these four, all fishermen, had known Jesus when they were in the Baptist's company. This explains why it was that when Jesus came to Galilee and, seeing these four in their fishing boats, called to them, "Follow me, and I will make you fishers of men," they at once left everything and followed him. They already had felt his commanding leadership and were ready to be his disciples.

Jesus' public work began so informally that the casual onlooker could not possibly have guessed what would come of it. One morning in Capernaum, where Jesus and his first disciples lived, the fishing boats came in and, as usual, a crowd gathered on the shore —customers looking for bargains in fish and curious folk wondering what the catch was. Suddenly a voice rang out. Jesus was speaking. The crowd need not have listened, but they could not help it. They thronged about Jesus until he was nearly forced into the water. So he stepped into a boat and, pushing off a bit from shore, spoke from the boat to the fascinated people.

The four fishermen were ready to be his disciples.

Of course the whole town soon heard of this new teacher. On one Sabbath day, therefore, when in the synagogue service the time came for what we call the sermon, Jesus was asked to speak. We are not told what he said, but Mark tells us how impressed the people were. "They were astonished at his teaching," Mark writes, "for he taught them as one who had authority, and not as the scribes." The scribes believed that God had revealed his whole will and purpose in the Old Testament, and that their official business was to teach the people what the Law and the prophets said. The scribes, therefore, often sounded to the common folk cold and formal. They reported at second-hand not what God was saying to them but what God long ago had said to someone else.

Jesus also loved and used the Old Testament but he spoke as though God was telling him directly what to say. He brought a vital message, out of his own experience. He told the people that the living God was going to establish His kingdom on earth, and that one by one they themselves could enter the kingdom now and so help to prepare the way for God's reign over all the nations. His message was personal, practical, applying to the daily life of the people, and he spoke with conviction as though he knew at first-hand the truth of what he said.

If ever you go to Capernaum you can see the foundations and the floor of that very synagogue where Jesus preached. It had been built for the Jews by a wealthy officer in the Roman army who worshiped Israel's God. It is an exciting experience to stand within that synagogue's walls, as I have done, and remember what happened there on that Sabbath long ago. For as Jesus was speaking, a crazy man, as we would describe him, interrupted Jesus, crying out, "What have you to do with us, Jesus of Nazareth? Have you come to destroy us? I know who you are, the Holy One of God."

If we are to understand what happened next, we must remember that in Jesus' time there was no such thing as scientific medicine. Many diseases, especially nervous troubles and upset minds, were supposed to be caused by demons who entered a man and lived in him. The only way to cure him was to drive the demon out. One favorite way of doing this was to beat and torture the man so that the demon would find his human dwelling place uncomfortable and move out. About thirty years ago an American scholar, traveling in Palestine, saw a crowd shouting and waving clubs at a man in the center of the group. One of the crowd, when he saw his chance, rushed up behind the man who was being beaten, seized his hands and tied them behind his back. When the American asked why the man was being so badly treated, he was told that the man had a demon which they were trying to drive out of him. There are many places on earth today where all sorts of diseases are thus explained as the work of "unclean spirits," and in Jesus' time everyone in Palestine believed this.

When, therefore, that mentally upset man disturbed the service in the Capernaum synagogue with his shouting, the people supposed he had a demon. That was familiar enough, but what happened next astonished them. Jesus stopped his sermon and, speaking to that supposed demon, said, "Be silent, and come out of him." And Mark tells us that the unclean spirit, "cry-

Jesus cured the man.

ing with a loud voice," did actually come out of him. That is to say, Jesus cured the man not by beating him up but by bringing his own powerful faith and the strength of God that was in him so to bear on that disturbed mind that the man regained his composure and sanity.

53

So, along with his teaching, which drew the crowds to hear him, Jesus' power of healing aroused intense popular interest. He was in the limelight now. In that Capernaum synagogue, Mark tells us, "They were all amazed, so that they questioned among themselves, saying, 'What is this? A new teaching! With authority he commands even the unclean spirits, and they obey him.' And at once his fame spread everywhere throughout all the surrounding region of Galilee."

Because in the end Jesus had so many enemies who at last crucified him, he is often spoken of as "despised and rejected of men." At the beginning of his ministry, however, far from being despised and rejected, he was about the most sensationally popular figure in Galilee. On the evening of that Sabbath when he healed the disturbed man in the synagogue, Mark tells us that "all the city was gathered at the door" of Simon Peter's house. Jesus was staying there, and "he healed many that were sick with various diseases and cast out many demons." Jesus' problem then was not rejection but popularity. And he was so troubled by it that early the next morning, before dawn, he slipped away alone and went to a "desert place" to pray.

Jesus had reason to be disturbed by this sudden popularity. A good deal of it was shallow. The crowds thronged about him not so much because they seriously welcomed the truths he was trying to teach them as because they loved to watch him work wonders, like casting out demons. Jesus had decided, when he was tempted in the wilderness, that he would not use his powers, like a magician, to amaze people and so make them follow him.

Others besides Jesus built up big reputations and sometimes gained wealth by working miracles—especially by driving devils out of people. Josephus tells about a Jew named Eleazar who thus gained distinction. Josephus actually saw him put on a wonderful show in the presence of Vespasian, the Roman Emperor. "The manner of the cure was this," says Josephus. "He put a ring . . . to the nostrils of the demoniac, after which he drew out the demon through his nostrils; and when the man fell down immediately, he adjured the devil to return into him no more."

Jesus, however, was no Eleazar. That was not what he had come for. He dreaded having people think of him as just a wonder-worker. He had come to save the souls of men, to transform their lives, to make God real to them, to prepare the way for a new kind of world in which justice and goodwill would reign. The last thing he wanted to be taken for was a man like Eleazar.

And yet here were these poor people whom he could help. He pitied them. His heart went out to the sick, to those tormented by anxiety and fear, to the mentally unbalanced. His compassion would not let him neglect their need. He cared for their bodies as well as their souls. So he did the best he could: he kept on healing people but he tried to make them keep still about it and not boast of him as a magician. Once, for example, after he had healed a leper, the first thing he said to the happy man was: "See that you say nothing to anyone."

Meanwhile Jesus launched a campaign that Mark tells us covered "all Galilee." From one village to another he went, preaching in the synagogues, speaking to the people in their homes, dealing with all kinds of personal problems that were brought to him. He was out to win the hearts of his people—especially those whom others neglected or even scorned. And he did win many of them with what he called "the good tidings of the kingdom of God."

As the number of his followers increased he looked for leaders among them. He wanted a small group of disciples whom he could train, so that they could be his special companions and helpers in his work. He started with the four fishermen and added eight more —all of them plain folk whom the so-called big men of the world would not have considered important at all. Imagine yourselves back there looking at those twelve disciples! A fisherman, Simon Peter, was as outstanding a person as any among them. Think of all the great men of the time—emperors and kings, high priests and scholarly rabbis, men of wealth and social standing in the vast Roman Empire—and compare them with this little band of Jesus' first disciples! Talk about a miracle! That little group was going to affect the future of the world more than any other people of their time. Simon Peter would turn out to be historically more influential than the Roman emperor. We would not have believed it then and we stand amazed at the thought of it now.

To be sure, Jesus' followers were multiplying. He was what we would call headline news in Galilee, and reports of him were traveling down the Jordan valley and up the hills to Jerusalem. "What is he up to?" the Jewish leaders began wondering. Critical, hostile eyes began watching him. He had become important and he needed watching, they thought. There was trouble ahead and it was not long in coming.

One sees the storm clouds on the horizon when Jesus called Matthew to be one of the twelve disciples. Matthew was a tax-collector. The Sea of Galilee was on the high road where traffic and trade flowed back and forth between the east and west, and the Romans made the most of it in collecting taxes on all that passed through. Can you imagine anyone more hated by the Jews than those tax-collectors, who gathered revenue for Rome and then some extra for themselves from their own countrymen? Yet Jesus called Matthew from his toll booth and he became one of the twelve disciples.

Moreover, Jesus dined at Matthew's house and many "tax gatherers and sinners," we read, ate with him. The strict scribes and Pharisees were disturbed. He actually likes sinners, they complained. He does not keep himself pure by avoiding tax gatherers and other unclean folk who do not observe our rules, they thought. Jesus' answer is one of the noblest things ever said in all man's history: "Those who are well have no need of a physician, but those who are sick; I came not to call the righteous, but sinners." This did not satisfy Jesus' critics, however, and it was clear that trouble was brewing for the Master and his followers.

4

WHY SOME PEOPLE HATED JESUS

In understanding the life of Jesus it is important to understand his enemies and why they hated him so much that at last they planned to kill him. From the beginning of his public ministry Jesus ran into trouble with the Pharisees. Many Christians today do not even try to understand the Pharisees, but simply condemn them for their hostility to Jesus. That, however, is not enough. We need to see what kind of people the Pharisees were, and why they were so honestly upset by Jesus' words and deeds.

The Pharisees were the most numerous party in Israel. As Josephus said, "The Pharisees have the multitude on their side." There was good reason for this popularity, for the Pharisees had saved the Jews from a great peril. The Jewish people might have been utterly crushed in war, but they had fought so bravely that they had escaped *that* fate. Another danger, how-

ever, threatened them, and it was this from which the
Pharisees saved them. The wealth, power and glory
of Greece and Rome might easily have so charmed
the Jews that they might have copied everything the
Greeks and Romans did and stopped being distinc-
tively Jews. That did happen to other peoples, who
took over the culture and customs of the Persians, the
Greeks or the Romans and, so losing their separate
existence, are now forgotten.

We all know that this did not happen to the Jews.
One of the marvels of history is the way the Jews have
survived as a distinct people, and the Pharisees deserve a large share of the credit for that achievement.
They insisted that a Jew must be unmistakably a Jew,
not only in what he believed, but in his clothes, his
food, his fasting, his observance of the Sabbath and
of all the rules drawn up to distinguish a Jew from
non-Jews. The very word Pharisee means "separatist,"
and the Pharisees did save the Jews from being swallowed up by foreign cultures and customs.

Anyone, however, can see the effect this had on the
Jewish religion of Jesus' day. Religion, as the Pharisees

understood it, concerned more than one's faith in God, one's habits in prayer and worship and one's good character. It concerned the way a person dressed and washed and ate, how he kept the rules of Sabbath observance, how he fasted, and how in daily life he kept clear of all trades and social contacts that the Pharisees called "unclean."

When once this way of conceiving religion got started, it kept piling up endless rules and regulations about everything, big and little. Here are a few samples of Pharisaic rules about Sabbath-keeping. A man might walk two thousand cubits—roughly three thousand feet—on the Sabbath, but no more. Some kinds of knots could be tied or untied on the Sabbath, but not others. Vinegar could be swallowed on the Sabbath to relieve a sore throat, but it could not be gargled. No woman could look in a mirror on the Sabbath lest, seeing a gray hair, she might be tempted to pull it out. No fire could be kindled on the Sabbath. A few years before Jesus' time two famous rabbis actually discussed and disagreed about the question whether an egg that a hen had laid on the Sabbath could be eaten. And the Pharisees had a whole set of rules about when and how a Jew should wash his hands, concerning which one rabbi wrote: "He who lightly esteems hand-washing will perish from the earth."

With this kind of petty religion Jesus was impatient. He called it "straining out a gnat and swallowing a camel." And the Pharisees reacted against his criticism with mounting hostility.

There are, therefore, two sides to the Pharisees. On one side they rendered magnificent service to the Jewish people, preserving their great traditions and saving them from becoming mere copies of the Greeks and Romans. On the other side, the method they used in doing this—laying down endless rules about every detail of daily life—often burdened their religion with trivialities.

Our Puritan forefathers in New England who founded Massachusetts Bay Colony faced this same kind of problem. They were sturdy men and women with strong religious convictions and magnificent courage, and we Americans owe them an unpayable

debt. But they too sometimes tried to protect their religion by little rules which some of them put on the
same level of importance with the really great matters
of Christian faith. As an example, one Puritan said
that to hold a wedding banquet on Sunday was "as
great a sin as for a father to take a knife and cut his
child's throat." And once, in Boston, Captain Kemble,
three years absent on a sea voyage and returning on
a Sunday, was greeted by his wife on their front door-
sill and, because he kissed her there in public, was
condemned to the pillory. Fastened by the neck and
wrists, he was exposed to the pity or the scorn of those
who passed by.

Of both the Puritans and the Pharisees, however,
it must be said that there were some among them
who disagreed with all this petty legalism. Indeed,
some of the Pharisees, far from hating Jesus, warmly
welcomed him. One of them even said to him, "Master,
I will follow you wherever you go." Mark tells us that
one Pharisee, hearing Jesus say that the first commandment is to love God and the second is to love
your neighbor as yourself, exclaimed, "You are right,

Teacher," and Jesus said to him, "You are not far from the kingdom of God." On three occasions Luke describes Jesus' dining in a Pharisee's home. And John's Gospel tells us that "a man of the Pharisees named Nicodemus" said to Jesus, "Rabbi, we know that you are a teacher come from God." Not all the Pharisees were against Jesus.

Nevertheless, Jesus was out to reform the religion of his people, and a conflict with the Pharisees was inevitable.

Here are a few incidents that show how this conflict started.

On one occasion when all good Jews were supposed to fast, the Pharisees saw Jesus and his disciples eating as usual. They complained about this. Jesus did not object to fasting if there was a real reason for it. He had gone without food himself when he was being tempted in the wilderness. But to fast as a matter of routine, just because the rules said one must not eat that day, was of no importance, Jesus thought. Indeed, it could mean putting on a pious show to make a man look religious. "When you fast," Jesus said once, "do not look dismal, like the hypocrites, for they disfigure their faces that their fasting may be seen by men." Anything like that Jesus scorned. So he did not observe the regular Jewish seasons of fasting, but said that his disciples were like a joyous wedding party, and that he was the bridegroom. "Can the wedding guests fast," he asked, "while the bridegroom is with them?" To the Pharisees, however, this meant that Jesus was being dangerously disloyal to Jewish laws.

On another occasion Jesus dined with a group of Pharisees, some of whom "had come from Jerusalem," probably to keep an eye on this dangerous man. At

Jesus dined with a group of Pharisees.

once they found something to complain about. Before dinner he and his disciples had not gone through the ceremony of hand-washing according to the detailed rules. "Why?" the Pharisees asked. "Why do your disciples not live according to the tradition of the elders, but eat with hands defiled?" Now Jesus doubtless had on his mind great matters concerning which he had wanted to talk that day—truths that would deepen the faith and redeem the character of Israel, and in the end bring God's kingdom to the whole world. And instead the Pharisees could think of nothing but a detail of hand-washing etiquette! Jesus was indignant. He called them "hypocrites"—that is, play-actors. He quoted Isaiah against them:

> "This people honors me with
>   their lips,
>   but their heart is far
>   from me."

He told them that they were neglecting the important matter, the real "commandment of God," and were putting all their emphasis on the customs of men. This, however, only made the Pharisees more sure that Jesus, if he had his way, would ruin their whole system of rules and regulations.

On another occasion Jesus spoke about the rules which the Pharisees tried to enforce concerning "clean" and "unclean" foods. These rules were a very important part of the Jewish law. Some foods—such as pork, which many people eat as a matter of course —no strict Jew would touch, and the rules went into great detail about just how everything eaten should be cooked. These rules were regarded as so important that even yet many of the Jewish people observe them carefully. When on the front of a butcher shop or a restaurant you see the word "Kosher," that means that everything sold there has been prepared according to the strict regulations of the old laws.

When Jesus brushed aside these rules about "clean" and "unclean" foods, you can imagine how outraged the Pharisees were. "Hear me, all of you, and understand," said Jesus. "There is nothing outside a man which by going into him can defile him; but the things which come out of a man are what defile him." As

Mark bluntly puts it, "Thus he declared all foods clean." This was so startling an idea that even his disciples were shocked, and when later they were alone with him they asked him to explain what he meant. Any wholesome food that a man eats, he told them, since "it enters not his heart but his stomach, and so passes on," cannot make a man bad or "unclean." What makes a man bad, he said, comes from within: "Out of the heart of man come evil thoughts."

To us this sounds like common sense, but to the Pharisees it meant that Jesus was breaking down the whole system of rules by which Jews were separated from Gentiles.

At no point did Jesus' words and actions disturb the Pharisees more than in his treatment of the Sabbath. One of the Ten Commandments says, "Remember the Sabbath day to keep it holy." That, however, raises the question: Just how does one keep the Sabbath holy? The Pharisees and their official scholars, the scribes, answered that question with a multitude of rules about everything that could be done or must not be done on the Sabbath. Now Jesus was a loyal Jew. He kept the Sabbath, as he had been trained to do from boyhood. He went to the synagogue on the Sabbath, "as his custom was," we are told, and doubtless he observed the sacred day in many ways that the Pharisees approved. But the strongest desire of his life was to help people, and he would not stop trying to do that on the Sabbath. If he saw anybody in need he helped him, and he could not imagine God wanting him not to do that because the chance came on the seventh day of the week. "It is right to do a kindness on the Sabbath," he said. And while that sounds innocent enough, it led him to do things that troubled the Pharisees.

Once, for example, a man with a "withered hand" was present at the synagogue service, and the Pharisees watched Jesus "to see whether he would heal him on the Sabbath, so that they might accuse him." Well, Jesus did heal him. According to the Pharisees that was work, and it was wrong to work on the holy day. Jesus had another point of view altogether. "Is it lawful on the Sabbath to do good or to do harm, to

73

save life or to kill?" he asked them. And when they simply glowered at him in silence, we read that "he looked around at them with anger." As for the Pharisees they were angry too, and began conspiring with the political followers of Herod Antipas to destroy him.

On another occasion, also in a synagogue on the Sabbath, Jesus healed a woman who, we read, "had had a spirit of infirmity for eighteen years." The head of the synagogue was indignant and told the people that there were six days in the week in which to work, and that they should not come even to be healed on the Sabbath. Jesus had a stinging answer for him. He said that each of them on the Sabbath untied his ox or his ass and led it away to give it water to drink, and "should not this woman, a daughter of Abraham," be helped also?

So Jesus, who believed with all his heart in keeping the Sabbath holy, broke free from the binding rules by which the Pharisees defined what that commandment meant. Once he and his disciples were walking along a path through some grain fields on the Sabbath and the disciples, being hungry, plucked a few ears of grain and, rubbing the chaff off with their hands, ate them. Some Pharisees who saw this were shocked. This was plainly working on the holy day. To Jesus, however, human need, like hunger, was more important than the Pharisees' rules. Jesus knew the Old Testament well, and he defended his disciples with a story about David. David, he reminded the Pharisees, when he was "in need and was hungry," once entered "the house of God," the temple, and actually ate the sacred bread which only the priests were allowed to eat and "also gave it to those who were with him." That is to say, genuine religion cares first of all about meeting real human need. It was after this incident that Jesus summed up the matter in one brief sentence: "The Sabbath was made for man, not man for the Sabbath."

This conflict between Jesus and the Pharisees was a tragedy. In some ways Jesus was closer to the Pharisees than to any other party in Israel. The Sadducees were priestly aristocrats in Jerusalem, co-operating

In a synagogue on the Sabbath, Jesus healed a woman.

with Rome, and in their religion they accepted as their Bible only the first five books of the Old Testament. They did not even believe in life after death. The Pharisees, on the other hand, were real patriots, their Bible was the whole of the Old Testament, and they did believe in life after death. Jesus was certainly on the Pharisees' side against the Sadducees. As for the Zealots, they stood for violent rebellion against Rome. The Pharisees rejected that, just as Jesus did.

If only the Pharisees could have seen how much they had in common with Jesus! Some of them did see that. In the early Christian church were men like Paul, whose letters make up a large part of the New Testament and who said once: "I am a Pharisee, a son of Pharisees." But the Pharisees, as a whole, were outraged by what Jesus said and did, and Jesus was indignantly impatient with their little rules. To him they seemed to be putting small things first and great matters last. You "have neglected the weightier matters of the law, justice and mercy and faith," he said.

So the tension grew more and more dangerous, as Jesus found himself deserted by the leaders of his people.

5

WHY CROWDS STILL FOLLOWED JESUS

To have the Sadducees, the Zealots and the Pharisees against him was trouble enough, but one of the hardest blows Jesus ever suffered was his own family's disbelief in him. His mother and his brothers loved him but, just because they loved him so much, they were frightened when they saw him trying to do what seemed to them impossible and stirring up such dangerous opposition. Mark tells us that Jesus' relatives actually said, "He is beside himself," or, as we might put it, "He is losing his mind." Once his mother and his brothers came to get him, and found him in a house so crowded with people that they could not come near him. When word was passed to Jesus that they were waiting outside, he knew that they had come to take him back to Nazareth. The time for a decision had come. If he was to go on with his God-given work, he would have to break with his family. It was one of the hardest decisions he ever made. "Who are my mother and my brothers?" he said to the people. "Whoever does the will of God is my brother, and sister, and mother." So he refused to go home with his family. John's Gospel says that "even his brothers did not believe in him." But we are glad to read that after his death among the disciples founding the first church were Jesus' mother and his brothers. One of the brothers, James, became an important leader.

But a crowd was around him that day when his family sought him—"so that they could not even eat," we read. Why, with the leaders in Israel turning against him, did this crowd of the common people still throng about him?

In John's Gospel we are told that once the multitude that followed him were ready "to take him by force to make him king." If someone says that this was written about 100 A.D. and exaggerates Jesus' popularity, the answer is to turn back to Mark, the earliest Gospel. There we read about "a great multitude" following him not only from Galilee and Jerusalem but from as far south as Idumea, from the cities beyond the Jordan to the east, and from Tyre and Sidon on the Mediterranean seacoast to the west. Moreover, we should remember that when, just before his crucifixion, Jesus made his spectacular entry into Jerusalem, which Christians still celebrate on Palm Sunday, "The crowds that went before him and that followed him" shouted "Hosanna" in welcome. In spite of all his enemies Jesus had a strong attraction still for the common people. Why?

One answer is that he himself was one of the common people. He had been a hard-working carpenter. He knew how ordinary folk thought and felt. He talked their language and drew his illustrations from their daily lives. The common people felt at home with him.

He said some things about their leaders that many of them had wanted to say but had not dared. Think what some of the Pharisees' rules about Sabbath-keeping must have meant to an ordinary, hard-working family! Only if a person was in danger of death

His family found him in a house crowded with people.

on the Sabbath was anything necessary to help him permitted to be done. If, on the other hand, a person broke his leg, nothing could be done about that till the Sabbath was over. If a man sprained his ankle, his wife could not even pour cold water on it until after the Sabbath sunset. A crowd always gathers to see a fight, and here was a man who had courage enough to fight the Pharisees, and to call silly many of their rules that the common people long had found oppressive.

Jesus stood up for the poor people against the rich, who often mistreated them. In one of his parables Jesus described "a rich man, who was clothed in purple and fine linen, and who feasted sumptuously every day. At his gate," said Jesus, "lay a poor man named Lazarus, full of sores, who desired to be fed with what fell from the rich man's table." There was a lot of that kind of thing in Jesus' day, as there is still, and Jesus' sympathy always went out to the distressed, the unfortunate, the poor. Some of the harshest things he ever said were his attacks on selfish, rich people. In one of his parables he described a wealthy landowner with a prosperous farm who thought of nothing except building bigger and bigger barns, and who said to his soul, "Soul, you have ample goods laid up for many years; take your ease, eat, drink, be merry." Jesus called him a "fool." And when he saw, as he did see, cruel mistreatment of plain people by the powerful, he exploded, as when he condemned those "who devour widows' houses and for a pretense make long prayers." Many of the common people must have felt that Jesus was on their side. He was their champion. This doubtless explains why some in the crowd followed him.

Another reason why so many common people followed Jesus lay in their curiosity about and their amazement at his miracles. Here we face a problem which troubles many people today and, if we are to understand it, we must consider the immense difference between the ideas about the universe which the people of Jesus' day held and the ideas which modern science has taught us.

In Jesus' day people thought the earth was flat. The sky was solid, like a bowl upside down, and the sun, moon and stars moved across the underside of this bowl to give light to man. Surrounding the earth and underneath it was the sea, and there was a sea above the sky too. Rain fell when these "waters which were above the heavens" came down through what the ancient people called "the windows of heaven." Inside the earth was a vast place called Sheol to which everyone went when he died, and where he stayed until the judgment day.

What a difference between that old view of the universe and the view which we hold now! But we moderns should not be scornful about that old view, two thousand years ago. What scientists will discover about our solar system and outer space in the next two thousand years will probably make our present views seem as queer to the people living in the year 3960 as the views of Jesus' day now seem to us!

One of the most important differences between the thinking of that ancient time and our scientific thinking is that then no one had ever dreamed of natural laws—such as the law of gravitation, for example. In the Old Testament we read that a prophet named Elisha made an axe-head float on water. When we read that we feel sure that it is impossible for an iron axe-head to float on water. But the writers of the Old and New Testaments had never imagined any such idea as laws of nature and, if they saw an axe-head float, they would not have said that it was impossible but that it was surprisingly unusual.

If we are to understand the stories of Jesus' miracles, we must try to put ourselves inside the minds of those ancient writers and to see things as they saw them. To them there were no laws of nature that made anything impossible. They told stories of Jesus walking on the water, feeding five thousand people with five loaves of bread and two fishes, stilling a tempest on the Sea of Galilee, changing water into wine, cursing a fig tree and making it wither, and even raising the dead. The ancient writers told these stories without being troubled by any such doubts as we moderns feel. To them such miracles were unusual, but they did not have in their minds any of our scientific ideas that would make such startling events seem impossible.

One result of the fact that in that ancient world natural laws were unknown was that all sorts of people, good and bad, were supposed to be able to work miracles. Many Christians today, when they think

about believing in miracles, limit the matter to believing in Jesus' miracles. No! The records of Buddhism, Judaism, and Mohammedanism are full of
accounts of miracles. A man named Apollonius, a con-
temporary of Jesus, had his biography written, and
the miracles he is said to have performed are strik-
ingly like those attributed to Jesus. In the Gospels
themselves we hear Jesus say that "false Christs and
false prophets will arise" and work miracles. Once
when his foes said that he cast out demons by the
power of a devil named Beelzebub, Jesus answered,
"If I cast out demons by Beelzebub, by whom do your
sons cast them out?" Many others performed miracles
besides Jesus.

That is one reason why, as we have seen, he kept
telling people to keep still about his miracles. He did
not want to be known as a magician or, as his enemies later called him, a "sorcerer." But the people
did not keep still. "He charged them to tell no one,"
says Mark after one miracle of healing, "but the more
he charged them, the more zealously they proclaimed
it."

Sincere Christians differ in their attitude toward the miracle-stories told about Jesus. Some Christians think that, because these stories are in the Bible, they must be taken literally and believed just as they were told by the ancient writers. Other equally devoted Christians think that, while many of these stories represent what actually happened, if a modern scientist had seen them happen, he would have described them in terms quite different from the terms which the ancient writers used.

Jesus' miracles of healing are the easiest to understand. Modern medicine has discovered that many diseases start not in the body but in the mind. The Yale University Out-Patient Medical Department recently reported that seventy-six per cent of all patients coming to that clinic are suffering from illnesses caused by unhealthy emotions such as anxiety, or resentment, or feelings of inferiority and guilt. Jesus undoubtedly did work marvelous cures. A modern physician would not describe those cures in the old term of casting out demons, but he would understand —especially if he were a neurologist or a psychiatrist

—how often health of body depends on health of mind. Jesus, with his God-given personal power, did heal many stricken folk when they had faith in him, and that was one reason why crowds followed him.

Concerning another kind of miracle, such as feeding five thousand people with five loaves and two fishes, each of us will have to make up his or her mind about what really happened. Some Christians believe the story just as it stands—as if by magic the few loaves and fishes were multiplied. Other Christians wonder whether, if they had been there, they would not have seen another kind of thing happen: Perhaps, at Jesus' suggestion, the disciples took their slender provisions and started sharing them with their neighbors. Seeing this, others began doing the same thing with the lunches they had brought, until at last all the crowd was fed. Equally sincere Christians differ in their interpretations.

In another miracle story Jesus, needing money to pay the required tax, told his disciples to go fishing, and said that they would find the needed coin in the mouth of the first fish they caught. Some Christians believe that this actually happened. Others think that the story is a picturesque way of describing an occasion when Jesus, needing tax-money, sent his disciples fishing, and they caught enough fish to pay the tax.

One of the most dramatic miracle stories told about Jesus describes an occasion when he came upon a really crazy man. Today we would call the man a homicidal maniac. His townsfolk feared him so much that they had driven him out to live "among the tombs." He himself said that not one demon but a whole legion of demons was in him. According to the story, when the demons saw that Jesus was going to drive them out of the man, they begged him to let them go into a herd of swine that was grazing near by. This, the record says, actually happened. Jesus cured the man, the demons went into the swine, and the swine "rushed down the steep bank into the sea, and were drowned." Some Christians believe that story literally, demons and all. Other Christians, who do not doubt in the least that Jesus cured the sick man, suspect that "crying out with a loud voice" the man himself frightened the swine so that they plunged into the sea.

In another miracle story we are told that one of the heads of the synagogue, Jairus by name, besought Jesus, saying, "My little daughter is at the point of death. Come and lay your hands on her, so that she may be made well, and live." Then, as Jesus was on his way to Jairus' home, messengers came saying that the girl had died. Jesus, however, went on to Jairus' house and said to the mourners there, who were weeping and wailing loudly, "Why do you make a tumult, and weep? The child is not dead but sleeping." They laughed at him, but he went to the bedside and, taking the child by the hand, said, "Little girl, I say to you, arise," and the child did arise. Some Christians think of this as raising the dead. Others think that Jesus was right; the girl was not dead but had fallen into what modern medicine calls a "coma," a state of unconsciousness, and they believe that Jesus healed her.

So one could go on and on, describing the different attitudes that equally sincere Christians take toward the miracles of Jesus. One thing, however, is certain: Jesus did do wonderful things in helping people, and the crowds followed him to see his marvelous deeds.

It is a strange fact that while the leaders of the three most powerful parties in Israel—the Pharisees, the Sadducees and the Zealots—were turning against Jesus, it still was true, as Mark tells us, that "the great throng heard him gladly." We have given various explanations of this fact, but there were some who followed Jesus for a deeper reason than we have yet spoken of. His disciples who knew him best— at first only a few men and women, but daily increasing in numbers—became more and more sure that Jesus was not just another prophet. One imagines them saying at first that God sent him. Then, as they saw more clearly and felt more strongly his divine quality and power, they went on to say that God was with him. Then, as his character and his teaching awakened their deepest reverence and awe, they began saying that God had come in him. It

94

Jesus told them, "The child is not dead but sleeping."

was this group who in the end founded the Christian church.

Jesus recognized the fact that all sorts of motives, some shallow and some deep, led the crowds to follow him. He told a parable in which he compared himself to a farmer who went out to sow his seed. Some seed, he said, fell on the hard path and was either trodden under foot or eaten by birds; some seed fell on rock and withered away; some seed fell among thorns and the thorns choked it. But some seed, said Jesus, "fell into good soil and grew, and yielded a hundredfold." So Jesus recognized that only a small part of the crowds that followed him would turn out to be "good soil."

6

JESUS FACES A DANGEROUS SITUATION

While many of the common people continued to believe in Jesus, the crowds were not always on his side. In his home town, Nazareth, he suffered a heartbreaking experience. While he was touring the villages of Galilee, he came one Sabbath to Nazareth, and was invited to read the Scripture and preach in the synagogue. At first, Luke tells us, his former townsfolk were impressed by what he said, but not for long. "Is not this the carpenter?" they said. What right had this humble workman to preach to them as he was preaching? They had heard with amazement and probably with disbelief stories of the marvelous deeds he had done in Capernaum and elsewhere, and Jesus could read their thoughts as they said to themselves, "What we have heard you did at Capernaum, do here also in your own country." They were not first of all interested in the truths he was trying to teach them. They wanted him to put on a show, to work miracles, and doubtless most of them did not believe that their former carpenter could do it. Jesus could not help people who had no faith in him, and so, as Mark tells us, "he could do no mighty work there."

That was a sad day for Jesus. He told the congregation, "Truly, I say to you, no prophet is acceptable in his own country." They were treating him, he said, just as their forefathers had treated the old prophets.

This was too much for the people of Nazareth. "They were all filled with wrath in the synagogue," Luke tells us, and seizing Jesus, they dragged him to the edge of the cliff on which the town was built, intending to "throw him down headlong." They did not actually do it, but they made it plain to Jesus that not only the leaders of Israel but even his own neighbors could turn against him. What a dreadful day that must have been for Jesus' family!

From that time on the heavy storm clouds gathered, threatening Jesus and his ministry.

100

One major danger that Jesus faced was the hostility of Herod Antipas, ruler of Galilee and of the lower Jordan valley. Herod was an evil man. He had lured his brother's wife, Herodias, away from her husband and had married her. As we have seen, John the Baptist condemned Herod for this, and Herod threw John into prison. Both Herod himself and es-

They dragged him to the edge of the cliff.

pecially Herodias held a bitter grudge against John but, fearing John's popularity with the multitude, they simply kept him in prison without putting him to death.

Then one night Herod threw a gay party to celebrate his birthday, and as his guests were eating and drinking the daughter of Herodias danced for them. Herod, who probably had drunk far too much, was delighted with her dancing, and he told her that she could have anything she asked of him, even to half of his kingdom. Salome—Josephus tells us that was her name—did not know what to request, and so she asked her mother. Herodias told her to ask Herod for the head of John the Baptist. When Herod heard this he was "exceedingly sorry," but what could he do? He would lose face with his dinner guests if he broke his promise. So he gave the order; John's head was cut off and presented to Salome.

This bloody deed haunted Herod's memory like a ghost. When later the news reached him that Jesus was working marvelous cures and drawing crowds after him, Herod's superstitious fears took possession of him. Who was this new troublemaker whom some called "a prophet, like one of the prophets of old," and others even called "Elijah"? Herod was sure he knew. "John, whom I beheaded, has been raised," he said.

So Herod ordered the arrest of Jesus. His officers teamed up with Jesus' other enemies, and it looked as though the end had come for the Master and his mission. Jesus, however, had friends even in Herod's court. One of the women who followed Jesus and contributed money to support his work was "Joanna, the wife of Chuza, Herod's steward." Perhaps she told Jesus that Herod was after him. Even some Pharisees said to him, "Get away from here, for Herod wants to kill you."

What was Jesus to do? The time had not yet come for him to die. His disciples needed longer training than he had given them. They did not understand his teaching well enough to carry on his work if he should be put to death then. So Jesus fled from the lands that Herod ruled.

Jesus fled from the lands that Herod ruled.

In those days there was a Roman road that ran from near Capernaum to Tyre, about thirty-five miles away, on the Mediterranean seacoast. Jesus escaped to Tyre by that road. We can see how serious he thought his danger was because even when he was safely out of Herod's territory he hid himself and "would not have anyone know it." Then he went

north to Sidon, then eastward through Dan and Caesarea Philippi, then south to the cities to the east
of the Sea of Galilee, all the way staying out of the
reach of Herod Antipas.

Evidently Jesus kept in touch with what his enemies were doing, for once he crossed the Sea of
Galilee by boat to the western side, where he was
again in Herod's territory. The Pharisees soon found
him, and began demanding from him what they
called "a sign from heaven"—that is, some startling
miracle which would prove that God had sent him.
To be sure, Jesus cured people, but the Pharisees
believed their own rabbis could do that. They wanted
another kind of "sign," such as, in the Old Testament story, Moses showed the people when he cast
his staff on the ground and it became a snake. Jesus
indignantly refused them. He could get nowhere
with them. He told them that no "sign" would be
given them. "He left them," we are told, "and get-
ting into the boat again he departed to the other
side."

So Jesus faced the increasing disbelief and hostility of his enemies—dangerous hostility that threatened his very life. The effect of this on Jesus' thinking about what was going to happen to him became clear in the famous conversation he had with his disciples one day near Caesarea Philippi. He asked them what men were saying about him. They answered that some people thought he was John the Baptist come to life again, and that others thought he was Elijah or one of the prophets. Then he asked them what they thought about him, and Peter said, "You are the Christ."

Matthew's Gospel tells us that Jesus warmly praised Peter, and said that on the solid rock of Peter's faith he would build his church. Nevertheless, as Matthew, Mark and Luke all agree, Jesus commanded the disciples not to tell anyone that he was the Christ. Once more he faced the disturbing fact that his idea of the Anointed One differed so widely from popular ideas of the Messiah that, if he used the title, it would only increase misunderstanding and distrust.

Then he began telling his disciples what was going to happen to him. "From that time," we read, "Jesus began to show his disciples that he must go to Jerusalem and suffer many things from the elders and chief priests and scribes, and be killed." That was a stunning blow to those disciples. They could not believe it. They had joined Jesus' company in the days of his popularity, when the crowds were following him. They had been thinking of the future not in terms of sacrifice and suffering but in terms of Jesus' victory, the glorious coming of God's kingdom, and honor and rich reward for Jesus' followers. And here Jesus was telling them that instead he was going to be killed. They could not believe that he really meant it. Peter exploded. He took Jesus, Matthew says, and "began to rebuke him," saying, "God forbid, Lord! This shall never happen to you." That was what Jesus himself had hoped too. In Peter's vehement outcry against the whole idea of a suffering and dying Messiah, Jesus felt himself facing his old temptation, and he said to Peter, "Get behind me, Satan!" For Jesus was now increasingly convinced that what lay ahead of him was suffering and death.

How had Jesus come to this strange idea of a suffering Messiah? Doubtless the growing hostility of his powerful enemies had helped to make his violent death seem probable. But the real explanation goes far deeper. In his fifty-third chapter the prophet Isaiah had described a true servant of God, who had saved his people by suffering for them. There can be no doubt that Jesus had thought long and deeply about passages like this from that chapter:

> *"He was despised and rejected by men;*
> *a man of sorrows, and acquainted*
> *with grief;*
> *and as one from whom men hide*
> *their faces*
> *he was despised, and we esteemed*
> *him not.*
> *Surely he has borne our griefs and*
> *carried our sorrows;*
> *yet we esteemed him stricken, smitten*
> *by God, and afflicted.*

But he was wounded for our trans-
gressions,
he was bruised for our iniquities;
upon him was the chastisement that
made us whole,
and with his stripes we are healed.
All we like sheep have gone astray;
we have turned every one to his
own way;
and the Lord has laid on him
the iniquity of us all."

So far as we know, no one before Jesus had ever
thought that Isaiah's portrait of a suffering savior
described the hoped-for Messiah. The Messiah had
commonly been pictured as a triumphant conqueror
of Israel's enemies. But Jesus was convinced of this
completely different idea of the Messiah. As he said,
he would "give his life as a ransom for many."

This is so important that we cannot understand
Christ or Christianity without seeing what it means
in terms of our own lives now. Dr. Albert Schweitzer
is one of the noblest men on earth today. He is a

great scholar and a great musician. He could have had a prosperous and easy life in his home country in Europe. But there was Africa, with its cruel diseases and poverty, calling him. So Dr. Schweitzer became a physician, went to Africa, founded a hospital there where he is bringing health and hope to the people, and where he will doubtless die that they may live. He illustrates one of the profoundest truths that Jesus taught and lived by. *Wherever men suffer from ignorance and sin there is only one way in which they can be saved: someone who does not have to do it, for the sake of those who do not deserve it, must voluntarily take on himself the burden of their need.* That principle Jesus accepted as the law of his life, and he foresaw that it meant that he would be "delivered into the hands of men, and they will kill him."

We can easily see what a staggering blow this was to the disciples. We read that "they did not understand the saying." Time and time again, in the weeks that followed, Jesus tried to make plain to them the kind of Christ he was—a savior, sacrific-

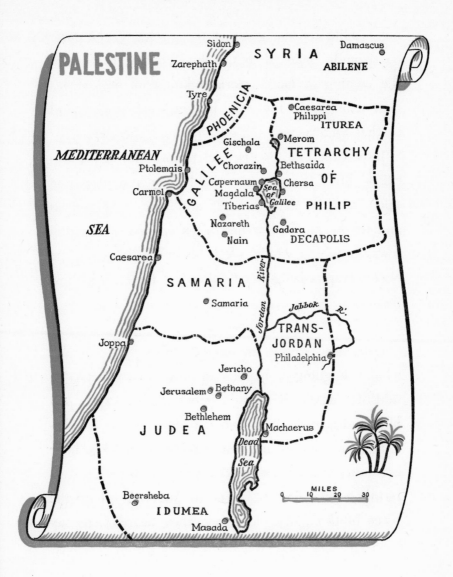

ing his life for the good of the world. To be sure, he strongly believed in the final victory of God, in the coming of God's glorious kingdom, and in his own triumph in the end, but meanwhile the road to that victory was self-sacrifice and the cross.

Jesus called on his disciples to join him in his sacrificial life. "If any man would come after me," he said, "let him deny himself and take up his cross and follow me." Jesus had often spoken of the rich rewards which would bless his followers. Now he began emphasizing what following him would cost them.

Jesus used strong language in telling his disciples what was going to happen to him and to them. He said that his enemies would "mock him, and spit upon him, and scourge him, and kill him." As for his disciples, John writes that Jesus said to them, "The hour is coming when whoever kills you will think he is offering service to God." Try to put yourself in the place of those disciples when they heard Jesus say things like that! They were perplexed and frightened. They tried hard not to believe what they heard him say. Would their faith and courage be sturdy enough to face such a test?

So Jesus set himself to strengthen them for the coming trial. About a week after he first told them that he was going to be killed, he took Peter, James and John up a high mountain and there he prayed. As he was praying, Luke tells us, "The appearance of his countenance was altered." What followed was one of those amazing experiences that, more than once, have changed the course of history. The disciples had a vision of their Master, his face and his very garments shining, and with him they saw Moses, the founder of the Jewish Law, and Elijah, first of the great prophets, talking. That is, they saw Jesus made glorious as the fulfillment of the Law and the prophets, and they were reassured and strengthened.

This story of what we now call the Transfiguration stands out uniquely in the Gospel's narrative, but surely it was only one of the ways by which Jesus deepened the faith of his disciples, shared with them the power of prayer, and prepared them for the costly sacrifice which lay ahead.

Meanwhile, Jesus was sure that the question whether his people would accept him or reject him could not be finally answered in Galilee. It must be answered in Jerusalem. He would go to Jerusalem. He would face the leaders of his people there in the holy city. Perhaps they would accept him but, if not, "it cannot be," he said, "that a prophet should perish away from Jerusalem."

Scholars differ about how long Jesus' public ministry lasted from the time he was baptized to the day he was crucified. Some think that it lasted less than a year; others say three years. And scholars differ too about whether Jesus had visited Jerusalem after his ministry in Galilee began. But all agree on Jesus' final deliberate decision to settle the matter of his acceptance or rejection by presenting himself to his people's leaders and to the throng of pilgrims in Jerusalem at

"The appearance of his countenance was altered."

the feast of the Passover. As Luke puts it: "He set his face to go to Jerusalem."

Meanwhile, he centered his attention on the training of his disciples. If he was to be killed, he must leave behind him a loyal group of men and women who understood him and believed in him. If they failed, his whole mission on earth would fail. He must prepare them not only for the suffering and sacrifice which awaited them but also for the heavy responsibility of carrying on his work. Everything depended on that.

7

JESUS TRAINS HIS
DISCIPLES

According to the Gospels Jesus was commonly addressed as "Teacher." He certainly was a teacher but, if he had been only that, he might have escaped serious trouble. The Jewish scribes and rabbis, who were also teachers, often differed sharply from one another and sometimes had hot debates. Jesus, however, was more than a teacher. He was a reformer. He was starting a revolution in Israel. He was out not simply to say something but to *do* something. His purpose was to organize a movement which would change and deepen the spiritual life of his people, which would bring out the best and get rid of customs and rules that did not really matter, and which in the end would have a gospel for all mankind. To this end he was gathering and training a devoted group of disciples, and was launching a campaign.

At the center of Jesus' followers were twelve men whom Jesus had chosen with the greatest care. Luke tells us that he prayed all night before he appointed them. Of the chosen twelve, eleven stood loyally by him and helped to found his church. Only Judas Iscariot, the traitor, failed him in the end.

To be sure, there were other disciples besides the twelve. Once Jesus sent out seventy of his followers, two by two, to preach his gospel and heal the sick. Luke tells us that after Jesus' resurrection about a hundred and twenty of his followers gathered in Jerusalem, and that because of their preaching the number soon rose to about five thousand.

The twelve men, however, whom Jesus especially depended on were the heart of his movement and, could we have seen them, we should have found it difficult to believe that they were going to change the course of history. Four of them were fishermen, one was a tax collector. They were all laymen; none of them had been trained for religious leadership; not a priest or a rabbi was among them.

Once, after Jesus' death, the Jewish leaders arrested

some of the disciples who were preaching about him. In the courtroom Peter and John fearlessly told them that "There is salvation in no one else." The Jewish leaders were astonished at the way these commonplace men stood up to them. "When they saw the boldness of Peter and John," Luke tells us, "and perceived that they were uneducated, common men, they wondered." Well, we still wonder!

We wonder all the more when we read the stories which they themselves told about their many failures to understand Jesus. Once, for example, he noticed that they were having a lively discussion among themselves. He asked them what they had been talking about. At first they would not tell him, but at last they did. They had been arguing about which of them was going to be the greatest when God's kingdom came. How completely their pride missed the spirit of Jesus! "If anyone would be first," he said to them, "he must be last of all and servant of all." Again and again Jesus tried to drive this lesson home. "Everyone who exalts himself will be humbled," he said, "but he who humbles himself will be exalted."

On Jesus' last journey to Jerusalem, he sent messengers ahead to a Samaritan village to find lodgings for the night. The Samaritans, however, who despised Jews just as Jews despised them, refused to let Jesus stay in their town. On hearing this, James and John lost their tempers. "Lord," they cried, "do you want us to bid fire come down from heaven and consume them?" Of course Jesus rebuked them. Were they never going to understand him? How often had he told them to love their enemies!

Nevertheless, on these disciples, who found it so difficult to understand their Master and to be like him, Jesus depended to carry on his work. We commonly think of the twelve as venerable saints. We see them in the stained glass windows of our churches—full-bearded, mature, even aged men. No! They were young men. Jesus himself was about thirty years old when he chose them, and they were probably no older. Some of them might have been much younger. To train these young men for the work that lay ahead was the central concern of Jesus, especially when he became sure that he was soon to die.

For one thing, he taught them to have faith that, even though they were "uneducated, common men," God could do great things through them. Anyone could see that they were very ordinary folk. They must often have felt that about themselves. What could they do? At times what Jesus expected of them must have seemed impossible. But Jesus shared with them his vigorous faith. "All things are possible with God," he said.

Once Jesus told them a story about a man who called his servants to him, and gave to one servant five talents, to another two, and to another one, "to each according to his ability." The five-talented man made five talents more; the two-talented man made four; but the one-talented man was discouraged, hid his talent, and did nothing with it. So men of small ability are always tempted to be discouraged about themselves and to leave their ability unused. When Jesus told that story, he surely was thinking of his disciples. They seemed to others and they must often have seemed to themselves to be one-talented men. But Jesus taught them that what they did with their small abilities was of immense importance. God could work wonders through them.

When those seventy disciples whom Jesus sent out on a preaching and healing mission returned, they were jubilant, because to their surprise they had been able to heal sick people and win followers for Jesus. Jesus was also joyful. He exclaimed, "I saw Satan fall like lightning from heaven!" That is to say, he foresaw that even through these men who seemed so commonplace God could win the victory over the world's evil.

So Jesus shared his faith with his followers until at last the disciples became the apostles, founders of the Christian church.

Another lesson that Jesus tried to teach his followers was as difficult for them to learn as it is for us, too. He said that ordinary sinners could love those who loved them, but that his disciples must do better than that. "Love your enemies," he said. "Do good to those who hate you, bless those who curse you, pray for

To train these young men was his central concern.

those who abuse you." One of our great American Negroes, Booker T. Washington, once said, "I will not let any man reduce my soul to the level of hatred." That was Jesus' spirit. He knew that his disciples were going to be hated and that they never could be his true followers if they hated in return. His whole movement depended on their being able to love their enemies.

That word "love" which Jesus used was not a soft word. It did not mean that the disciples were to like their enemies and feel affectionately about them. But it did mean that when they faced ill will they should meet it with good will. His gospel could never win the world by violence, war, or hatred, but only by endless good will that kept on loving people even when they were hostile.

So Jesus taught his disciples never to hold a grudge, never to try to "get even," never to hit back. Peter asked him once, "Lord, how often shall my brother sin against me, and I forgive him?" Then, doubtless thinking himself very generous, Peter added, "As many as seven times?" But Jesus was not satisfied with that. "I do not say to you seven times," he said, "but seventy times seven." Their good will, Jesus tried to teach his disciples, must be endless and undiscourageable. He told them a story about a master who forgave a servant a huge debt of twelve million dollars. Then this servant, who had been forgiven so much, went out and found a fellow-servant who owed him a tiny debt—only seventeen dollars—and, seizing him by the throat, cried, "Pay what you owe."

Don't be mean like that, Jesus counseled; think what God has forgiven you, and always be ready to forgive others.

Jesus was not a soft man. He could be terrific in his indignation against evildoers. But even on the cross his good will went out to those who crucified him, and he prayed, "Father, forgive them, for they know not what they do." Years afterward, when Peter was writing a letter to the churches, he remembered most of all this spirit of his Master, and wrote about him, "When he was reviled, he did not revile in return; when he suffered, he did not threaten." Such endless good will Jesus tried to inspire in his disciples.

Another difficult lesson which Jesus taught his disciples was to care especially for people whom others neglected and despised. There were many Jews who had stopped even trying to keep all the little rules of the Pharisees, and the Pharisees looked down on them, calling them "sinners" and refusing to associate with them. "This crowd," they said, "who do not know the law, are accursed." Jesus' attitude was exactly the opposite. "When he saw the crowds," Matthew tells us, "he had compassion on them, because they were harassed and helpless, like sheep without a shepherd."

Read the fifteenth chapter of Luke's Gospel. Tax collectors and sinners, outcasts whom the Pharisees despised, were around Jesus, and he was even eating with them. When the Pharisees saw this, they scornfully condemned him. Then Jesus told three of his most wonderful parables, about the lost sheep, the lost coin and the Prodigal Son. Jesus was saying, in effect, that God cares especially about these outcast people whom the Pharisees despised—cares about every one of them—so that "there is joy before the angels of God over one sinner who repents." Just as a doctor

He had compassion on the harassed and helpless.

cares especially for sick folk whom he can cure, so Jesus cared especially for bad folk whom he could save.

This flaming faith of Jesus that no one need stay the way he is, that he can be changed, that the bad can be made good, Jesus tried to share with his disciples. They actually saw him changing people's lives and characters. Mary Magdalene, so hopeless that tradition says seven devils were cast out of her, became one of his most faithful disciples. Zacchaeus, a dishonest tax collector, was so changed after Jesus got hold of him that he said, "Behold, Lord, the half of my goods I give to the poor; and if I have defrauded anyone of anything, I restore it fourfold." The Prodigal Son in Jesus' story was typical of what the disciples saw happening all through Jesus' ministry. That boy had made a sorry mess of his life, finally landing in a foreign country where he fed swine. But he came home again, and his father received him, saying, "This my son was dead, and is alive again; he was lost and is found."

This faith of Jesus that bad people could be saved

was contagious, and the disciples caught it. Jesus not only said that he "came to seek and to save the lost," but he practiced it so amazingly that the disciples made that the cardinal message in the early church. It was a Jewish scholar, Dr. Kohler, who said that "the chief cause of the triumphant power of the Christian church" was the fact that the early Christians broke free from the "contemptuous and hostile attitude of the Pharisaic schools toward the masses," and went out into the world with the gospel that lost men and women could be found and saved.

There was another lesson which Jesus tried to teach his disciples and which they found it hard to accept and practice. He was against what we call "racial prejudice." He believed that God was the Father of all men and women of all races and nations. When God's kingdom came he did not think it would be only for Jews. He pictured men and women from everywhere enjoying God's victory. "Many will come from east and west," he said, "and sit at table with Abraham, Isaac and Jacob."

Jews, for example, commonly despised Samaritans. One of Jesus' most famous parables, however, is about a good Samaritan. A traveler—probably a Jew—was on his way from Jerusalem to Jericho, he said, when robbers stripped him, beat him, and left him half dead. A Jewish priest who saw the victim passed by without helping him. Then a Jewish Levite—one who took an important part in the temple services—did the same thing. But when a Samaritan saw the wounded man, he helped him, said Jesus, bound up his wounds, put him on the Samaritan's donkey, carried him to the nearest inn and, when he left the next day, paid the innkeeper to take care of him.

Jesus had no prejudices which made him dislike Samaritans just because they were Samaritans, or foreigners just because they were not Jews. Every man, in Jesus' thinking, would be judged for what he himself was, not for the race or nation he came from. Once when he healed a Roman centurion's servant, he was so impressed by the Roman officer that he exclaimed, "Not even in Israel have I found such faith."

132

Of course, Jesus knew that in his short lifetime he must center his attention on his own people. When he first sent his twelve disciples out on a preaching mission, he told them to go only to "the lost sheep of the house of Israel." That was the place where he and his disciples had to begin. But it was not the place where they were to end. "The field is the world," he said, and, "You are the light of the world." So he tried to prepare his disciples to do what they did do after he was gone—carry his gospel to the ends of the earth.

It would be unfair of us to suppose that Jesus' care for the Gentiles—the foreign peoples who were not Jews—was not shared by the best of the Jews also. In one Jewish book, *The Testament of the Twelve Patriarchs*, we read: "The Lord shall reveal his salvation to all Gentiles" and "The Lord shall visit all Gentiles in his tender mercies forever."

But racial prejudice was dreadfully strong then, as it is now, and it took a long time and a hard struggle before those disciples learned to eat with Gentiles, treat them as equals, and welcome them freely into the fellowship of the church. On that road Jesus started his disciples, and for that end he tried to train them.

Jesus and his disciples were sustained in all their difficulties by the faith that, no matter how hard the going was, God in the end would win the victory. When Jesus taught his disciples the Lord's Prayer, he put this petition first: "Thy kingdom come, Thy will be done, on earth as it is in heaven." They all believed that that prayer would be answered. This was one lesson which Jesus had no trouble teaching his followers. They had been brought up from childhood to believe that God in the end would overthrow His enemies and establish His kingdom.

There were different ideas about what that kingdom would be like, and about when it would come. Luke tells us that the disciples "supposed that the kingdom of God was to appear immediately." The most important thing which Jesus said about the time of the kingdom's coming was that no one knew the time, not even the angels or Jesus himself, but God only. Once, when the Pharisees asked him when God's great victory would come, he answered that "the kingdom of God is in the midst of you," or, as Jesus' words may be translated, "is within you."

That was Jesus' main emphasis. God now can establish His rule in your hearts, he said. Now you can enter the kingdom. Now you can become "sons of the kingdom." You cannot know when God's final victory over the whole world will come, he said, but God can now win the victory in your lives. And lives where God has won the victory are like yeast, he said, which works secretly until all the dough becomes bread.

So Jesus trained his disciples. No hardship could discourage him. He was a radiant personality. No matter how dismaying the circumstances were, he was sure that "Every plant which my heavenly Father has not planted will be rooted up." Even in the darkest days he could say to his disciples, "Be of good cheer."

8

JESUS CHALLENGES
JERUSALEM

Jesus did one of the bravest deeds ever done on earth when he gathered his followers around him and began his last journey to Jerusalem. He felt sure that the great decision could no longer be postponed— his people were going either to accept him or reject him. At the feast of the Passover not only would his enemies be in Jerusalem, but great crowds of pilgrims also, many of whom were his friends. Perhaps they might swing the decision in his favor. Jesus did not expect that, but at any rate he was going to force the issue.

As he drew near Jerusalem he stopped at Bethany, a half hour's walk from the city, and made his headquarters at the home of a friend called Simon the leper. There he planned a dramatic entry into the city. One of the Old Testament prophets, Zechariah, had described the Messiah's coming to Jerusalem humbly

riding on a colt. That Jesus' entry might be in keeping with that prophecy two of his disciples went
ahead and found a young donkey. They threw their
cloaks on its back and Jesus mounted it and rode into
the city, surrounded by a great crowd. Some spread
their garments on the road for him to ride over, and
others spread "leafy branches which they had cut
from the fields." And all the crowd, Mark tells us,
cried: "Hosanna! Blessed be he who comes in the
name of the Lord! Blessed be the kingdom of our
father David that is coming! Hosanna in the highest!"

That was an exciting welcome which Jesus received
from his followers. It is still celebrated on what we
call Palm Sunday. It must have thrilled his disciples.
Could it be that, after all, Jerusalem would accept
his leadership? John's Gospel tells us that the Pharisees were badly upset, and said to one another, "You
see that you can do nothing; look, the world has gone
after him."

That afternoon Jesus went into the temple and
"looked around at everything," doubtless planning

He came to Jerusalem humbly riding a donkey.

what he was going to do there the next day. Then he
went out to Bethany to spend the night. The following morning, Monday, he came back to the city and
went to the temple, determined to challenge the
leaders of his people with a daring act which would
force them either to recognize his authority or else
utterly reject him. When one entered the temple, one
first came to the Court of the Gentiles, a spacious hall
where men and women of all nations could worship.
Then came another court reserved for Jewish women,
and then a court reserved for Jewish men. Beyond
that was the Court of the Priests, where none but
priests could come, and beyond that was the curtained
sanctuary, the central shrine of the Jewish religion.
Jesus' indignation that morning was aroused by what
he saw going on in the Court of the Gentiles.

There the moneychangers were busily at work,
taking from the pilgrims the various kinds of money
they had brought from their homelands, and giving
them in exchange the sacred coins which alone were
allowed in the temple to purchase animals for sacrifice.
And there too were the animals, from bullocks and

rams to doves and pigeons, on sale for all who wished to buy. And back and forth, using the Court of the Gentiles as a short cut, men were carrying their burdens. To Jesus all this was intolerable.

The reason for Jesus' indignation was not only that turning the temple into a banking house and an animal market shocked him, but also that so much of the business going on there was downright dishonest. The temple traders had set up a monopoly and were cheating the people. The moneychangers did not give the sacred shekels to the pilgrims in exchange for their foreign currencies without making a good profit. As for those who sold sacrificial animals, they could overcharge the pious pilgrims, because animals bought in the temple were guaranteed to be free from all defect, while any animal purchased elsewhere had to be passed on by censors, who easily could find some defect in them. Four cents apiece was the usual price for pigeons then, but it is on record that once the temple traders charged $3.90 for two pigeons.

So Jesus indignantly cleansed the temple. He drove out those who were buying and selling in the Court of the Gentiles. He upset the tables of the money-changers and overturned the booths of those who sold pigeons. And, as he did this, he cried, "Is it not written, 'My house shall be called a house of prayer for all the nations'? But you have made it a den of robbers."

Of course, Jesus could not have done this single-handed. The common people were back of him. The crowd was on his side. The chief priests were furious at him and "sought a way to destroy him." But, so Mark tells us, "they feared him, because all the multitude was astonished at his teaching," or, as another translation puts it, "his teaching had captured the imagination of the people."

After that daring act of Jesus' in cleansing the temple, his enemies redoubled their efforts to destroy him. At first they tried to trap him into saying something which they could use as a legal charge against him, or which would turn his friends away from him. They asked him by what authority he did what he was

Jesus drove out the moneylenders.

doing, hoping that he would give an answer that would seem proud and blasphemous. He replied that he would not answer their question until they answered one of his. Was the ministry of John the Baptist, he asked them, inspired by God or not? That stumped them, for if they said that John the Baptist was inspired by God, the people would ask them why they had not accepted and followed John; and if they said that John was not divinely inspired, that would anger the people, who believed that John was a real prophet. So they dodged the issue and said, "We do not know." Thus their first attempt to trap Jesus hurt them rather than him.

Again they tried to trick Jesus by flattering him, telling him that they knew he was a fearless teacher who truly taught "the way of God." Then they asked him, "Is it lawful to pay taxes to Caesar or not?" That was a dangerous question. If Jesus said that it was right to pay the Roman taxes he would enrage the Jewish patriots, and if he said that it was not right to pay them, the Roman government might be persuaded to arrest him. Jesus, however, saw through their trickery and said, "Bring me a coin, and let me look at it." So they brought him a silver coin about the size of our ten-cent piece, with the profile picture of the Roman Emperor Tiberius upon the face of it. "Whose likeness and inscription is this?" he asked, and they answered, "Caesar's." Then Jesus made a famous statement which baffled his enemies, because they could not use it against him one way or another, but which ever since has helped devout people in their thinking about their duties to church and state. "Render to Caesar," he said, "the things that are Caesar's, and to God the things that are God's." So again and again Jesus' enemies tried to trap him, and failed.

Meanwhile, he went on teaching his disciples and all who would listen to him. Once in the temple he watched the pilgrims putting their contributions into the trumpet-shaped receptacles that stood in the Court of the Women. The rich put in their large gifts, but when Jesus saw a poor widow shyly drop in "two copper coins, which make a penny," he called his disciples to him, and pointing her out to them, said that she had put in more than all the others. They had given out of their wealth, he said, but "she out of her poverty has put in everything she had." This special care of Jesus for the humble and the poor had run through all his ministry and now, at the end, it was strongly evident. Despite the fact that he knew himself to be God's Anointed One, he too was humble. On that last journey to Jerusalem, a man ran up to him and, kneeling, called him "Good Teacher." Jesus said, "Why do you call me good? No one is good but God alone."

This spirit of Jesus was beautifully expressed in the last parable he ever told. Turn to the Gospel of Matthew, the twenty-fifth chapter, beginning at the thirty-first verse, and read it for yourselves. Jesus pictured the last judgment as the Jews commonly thought of it, with the Messiah on his throne separating the good people from the bad. Who were the good souls whom the King welcomed into his eternal kingdom? They were those who had fed the hungry, had given drink to the thirsty, had welcomed strangers, clothed the naked, and visited the sick and imprisoned. "Truly I say to you," Jesus taught his disciples, "as you did it

Judas Iscariot offered to betray Jesus.

to one of the least of these my brethren, you did it to me."

While this gracious side of Jesus' teaching was clearly evident during those last days in Jerusalem, the stern side was evident also. Never had he spoken more harshly about the hypocrisy of his people's religious leaders. "Beware of the scribes," he said, "who like to go about in long robes, and to have salutations in the market places and the best seats in the synagogues and the places of honor at feasts, who devour widows' houses and for a pretense make long prayers. They will receive the greater condemnation." We can easily imagine how the hatred of his enemies grew hotter every day. "They tried to arrest him," says Mark, "but feared the multitude."

Then the break came, the chance that in their wildest dreams his enemies could hardly have hoped for: Judas Iscariot, one of Jesus' disciples, went to the chief priests and offered to betray him.

Why did Judas betray Jesus? Was it because he was a greedy man who loved money? Did he turn traitor just to get the thirty pieces of silver which the priests paid him? But those thirty pieces of silver were worth in our money no more than twenty dollars. Moreover, when the Jewish elders and chief priests had condemned Jesus, bound him, and taken him to the Roman governor, Pontius Pilate, to be tried and put to death, Judas was horrified at what he had done. He took the thirty pieces back to the priests, crying, "I have sinned in betraying innocent blood." And when they brushed him off, saying, "What is that to us? See to it yourself," Judas threw down the bribe money on the floor, and went out and hanged himself. So it is difficult to be satisfied with the idea that Judas turned traitor just for money.

Perhaps there had been a quarrel among the disciples, some have thought, and Judas was peeved and angry. He was the only disciple who was not a Galilean. He came from Judea. His dialect was different from the others'. Perhaps he felt at odds with them and, after a quarrel, decided that he did not belong in their company. This is only a guess, however, and is not at all convincing.

Others have thought that Judas was really a loyal disciple, but was impatient because Jesus seemed to him to be dillydallying instead of using his divine power to strike down his enemies and bring in the

Messianic kingdom. What if Judas could bring the crisis to a head, could create a situation where Jesus would *have* to act? *That* would force Jesus—so Judas may have thought—to reveal his heavenly power and decide the issue once for all. This also is a guess. No one knows what really was Judas' reason for turning traitor.

Meanwhile Thursday had come, and that evening Jesus and his twelve disciples ate the Passover supper together. Could we have seen that little group about the table, we might easily have turned away, quite unaware that anything of great importance was happening there. But now, centuries afterward, we still celebrate in our churches that last supper which the Master ate with his disciples. To millions of Christians around the world the Lord's Supper is the most sacred occasion in the church's worship. We remember then with reverent gratitude the sacrifice he made for all of us. For, while they were eating, Jesus took bread and, having blessed it, he broke it into small pieces and gave it to his disciples, saying, "Take; this is my body." And after that

He and his disciples ate the Passover supper together.

he poured wine into a cup, and gave it to them, say-ing, "This is my blood of the covenant, which is poured out for many." How little they understood what was really happening there! Judas was present; he did not understand at all. And none of them could have guessed what that supper was going to mean as long as the world lasts.

After the supper they sang a hymn and then went out to the Mount of Olives, to a place called Gethsem-ane. This gave Judas his chance. Luke tells us that Jesus went to Gethsemane "as was his custom." It was a lovely place where he could quietly think and pray under the olive trees. Judas, therefore, knew it well, and it fitted his plan perfectly, for there the chief priests could arrest Jesus secretly. That was what Judas had promised the priests: "to betray him to them in the absence of the multitude." That was what Jesus' enemies wanted: "to arrest him by stealth . . . lest there be a tumult of the people." So Judas slipped away from the supper to tell the chief priests where Jesus was going.

When Jesus went to Gethsemane that night he knew that death awaited him. His heart was heavy with sorrow and anxiety, not only for himself but for his disciples as well. Would they rise above the shock of his crucifixion and be brave and faithful in carrying on his work? He quoted to them the words of the prophet Zechariah, "I will strike the shepherd, and the sheep will be scattered." To be sure, Peter at once protested that, though all the rest failed him, he would not. When Jesus told him that that very night, before the cock crowed at dawn, he would deny his Lord, Peter cried, "If I must die with you, I will not deny you." Nevertheless, Jesus knew how unprepared the disciples were to face what was going to happen. "My soul is very sorrowful," he said, "even unto death."

Under the olive trees he left eight of the disciples and, taking Peter, James and John with him, he went farther into the wood. Then, telling them to watch, he went on alone to pray in solitude. He fell on the ground, Mark tells us, and prayed that if it were possible he might escape the cruel fate his enemies planned for him. "Abba, Father," he said, "all things are possible to Thee; remove this cup from me; yet not what I will, but what Thou wilt." Three times he prayed thus, and each time, when he returned to his three disciples, he found them sleeping. "Simon," he said to Peter, "are you asleep? Could you not watch one hour?" So with a heavy heart he waited for the blow to fall.

Suddenly Judas appeared, followed by a crowd armed with swords and clubs. The chief priests had been delighted at the news Judas had brought them. Now they were seizing Jesus in the darkness of night, when the multitude of his friends could not know and could start no riot. The traitor had told the armed band which followed him that he would kiss Jesus and so show them the one they were to arrest. That shameful thing he did. He went directly up to Jesus and, calling him "Master," kissed him. Then the armed men seized Jesus and took him away to the high priest, while the disciples "all forsook him and fled."

One wonders what Jesus was thinking as his rough captors dragged him away to his trial and crucifixion. One suspects that he was concerned not so much about

He prayed in solitude.

himself as about his disciples and his nation, the Jewish people whom he loved. He had come to their holy city to face them with the most important decision they had ever made, and now their fatal choice was clear. The words which he had spoken only a day or two before may well have been again in his mind: "O Jerusalem, Jerusalem, killing the prophets, and stoning those who are sent to you! How often would I have gathered your children together as a hen gathers her brood under her wings, and you would not! Behold your house is forsaken and desolate."

9

JESUS' TRAGEDY AND TRIUMPH

Ordinarily the high priest would not have called his council together in the middle of the night, but that Thursday Caiaphas—that was the high priest's name —was in a hurry. He wanted to have Jesus crucified on Friday, and so get the whole bothersome business over and done with before Saturday, the Jewish Sabbath. When, therefore, Judas promised that Jesus would be seized in Gethsemane, Caiaphas gathered his council together so that they could try him and condemn him that very night.

The high priest's council was called the Sanhedrin. It had seventy members, but when it sat as a court to try anyone only twenty-three had to be present. There they were in Caiaphas' palace that Thursday night waiting for Jesus to appear, and we can easily imagine how happy they were when the soldiers brought him in and they knew that their conspiracy with Judas had worked out well.

The Sanhedrin did not have the power to condemn anyone to death. Only the Roman governor could do that. What the Sanhedrin wanted to do was to find some evidence against Jesus that would make him look dangerous to the Romans. Then they could carry him to Pontius Pilate, the Roman governor, and demand his death. Caiaphas and his fellow-councilors, however, ran into difficulty. They had picked up all the witnesses they could find to give damaging testimony against Jesus, but no two of them agreed. One of the Sanhedrin's rules was that no one could be sentenced to death unless two witnesses gave the same testimony against the accused man. For a while that night the Sanhedrin were completely at a loss. "Many bore false witness against him," Mark tells us, "and their witness did not agree." And all the while, with one false accusation after another being hurled against him, Jesus stood there silent. One wonders if he was thinking of that verse in Isaiah's great chapter about the suffering savior:

*"He was oppressed, and he was
afflicted,
yet he opened not his mouth."*

This silence of Jesus provoked Caiaphas. "Have you no answer to make?" he shouted. But still Jesus said nothing. Then Caiaphas played his trump card. Judas probably had told the priests that Jesus claimed to be the Messiah. If only Caiaphas could get Jesus to say that he was the Messiah, that would settle the matter. As the Romans saw it, the Jewish Messiah was bound

Jesus stood silent before the Sanhedrin.

to be a troublemaker, stirring up a revolution against Roman rule. So Caiaphas faced Jesus and said, "Are you the Christ, the Son of the Blessed?" and Jesus said, "I am." Then Caiaphas in a fury tore his own clothes and cried, "Why do we still need witnesses? You have heard his blasphemy. What is your decision?" The Sanhedrin was unanimous—they all voted that Jesus deserved to die.

While all this was going on, something was happening to Peter which he never could forget. When the disciples fled from Gethsemane, Peter had followed at a distance the guards who had captured Jesus. He saw them go into the high priest's palace. Then when the guards had turned Jesus over to the Sanhedrin and were sitting around a fire in the courtyard, Peter slipped in among them and sat there watching. Soon one of the maids in the high priest's household saw him warming himself and said to him, "You also were with the Nazarene, Jesus." That scared Peter, and he told the maid that he did not even understand what she meant.

Fearful of being discovered, Peter left the fire and "went out into the gateway." There the maid saw him again, and began pointing him out to the bystanders as one of Jesus' company. Peter stoutly denied it. In denying it, however, he gave himself away, for the bystanders recognized his Galilean accent. "Certainly you are one of them," they said, "for you are a Galilean." Then Peter began to curse and swear, crying, "I do not know this man of whom you speak."

At just that moment a rooster crowed. That meant nothing to the others, but it meant a lot to Peter. For when in Gethsemane Peter had protested to Jesus that though all the others denied him, he never would, Jesus had told Peter that before the cock crowed that coming morning he would deny his Master three times. Poor Peter! Remembering Jesus' words, and thinking of what he had just done, he left the high priest's palace and "broke down and wept."

Years afterwards Simon Peter and John Mark were friends and companions. The record of Peter's denial of Jesus in Mark's Gospel must be the story as Peter himself told it to his friend.

At sunrise the Sanhedrin met again, confirmed their decision made at the night meeting, bound Jesus, and carried him to Pontius Pilate's palace. There they accused Jesus of disturbing the nation, of telling the people not to pay the Roman taxes, and of calling himself "Christ, a king." They were putting their accusations in a form most likely to make Pilate angry. Pilate, however, looked at Jesus in his humble peasant's clothes and asked him, "Are you the King of the Jews?" He probably spoke sarcastically, and Jesus answered him accordingly, "You have said so."

Pilate was favorably impressed by Jesus. During his few years as Roman governor he had had all sorts of trouble with the Jewish leaders, and he did not trust them. Here they were accusing this humble, quiet man of being a dangerous rebel, of stirring up the people against Rome and calling himself a king; and here was Jesus refusing to say a word in answer. Luke tells us that "Pilate marvelled" at this quiet dignity of the accused man. So, after a while, Pilate said to the chief priests and the bystanders, "I find no crime in this man." But his accusers insisted that Jesus had made himself a public danger all the way from Galilee to Jerusalem.

That gave Pilate an idea. So Jesus was a Galilean! Pilate knew that Herod Antipas, ruler of Galilee, had come to Jerusalem for the Passover festival. This so-called dangerous rebel was Herod's responsibility, Pilate thought; let him handle the case! So Jesus and his accusers were sent to Herod. The ruler was delighted to see this man whom he hated, and was doubtless delighted too to see him in such desperate trouble. Herod questioned Jesus "at some length," Luke tells us, but Jesus answered him not a word. Now Herod, who knew how many friends Jesus had in Galilee, much preferred to have Pilate take the blame for his death. So he and his soldiers, having treated Jesus with contempt and mockery, dressed him up "in gorgeous apparel" to make fun of his kingship, and sent him back to Pilate.

Pilate, however, still not wishing to condemn Jesus to death, tried another way of escape. The Roman governor, Mark says, was accustomed at the Feast of the Passover to release from prison some man whom the people especially wanted set free. That Friday morning a crowd had come to Pilate's court to ask for a prisoner's release. Pilate thought he saw his chance. Here was Jesus, being called "the King of the Jews." Let me set *him* free, said Pilate to the people. But the chief priests persuaded the crowd to demand the release of Barabbas, "who had committed murder in the insurrection." And when baffled Pilate asked them what he should do with the man they called the King of the Jews, the crowd, spurred on by the chief priests, shouted again and again, "Crucify him!" Pilate protested, "Why, what evil has he done?" But the crowd all the more cried out for his crucifixion, until Pilate, "wishing to satisfy the crowd," set Barabbas free and condemned Jesus to the cross.

Matthew alone tells us that before Pilate made this fatal and cowardly decision, "he took water and washed his hands before the crowd, saying, 'I am innocent of this man's blood; see to it yourselves.'" History has disappointed Pilate's hopes. It takes more than a basin of water to clear the man who sentenced Jesus to death.

Pilate condemned Jesus to the cross.

In those cruel days a man condemned to be crucified was first of all flogged—brutally beaten with leather whips—and Pilate saw that this was done to Jesus. Then the Roman soldiers took him into their courtyard and, knowing that he was accused of calling himself "King of the Jews," they put a purple robe on him, made a wreath out of a thorny vine and crowned him with it, put a stick in his hand to represent a royal scepter and, kneeling down, boisterously mocked him with cries of "Hail, King of the Jews." When they were tired of that, they took the stick out of Jesus' hand and began beating him on the head with it and spitting on him. Then they put his own clothes on him and marched him outside the city walls to the place of crucifixion called Calvary.

We often see pictures of Jesus on that dreadful march, carrying his cross—an upright beam with a crossbeam attached to it at right angles. Almost certainly that is not what actually happened. The upright beams were already firmly planted in the ground at Calvary, and what Jesus had to carry—like the others who were crucified with him—was the crossbeam. Even this, however, was more than Jesus could endure. He had had no sleep the night before, and he was so weakened by the brutal flogging that he fell beneath the load. So the soldiers compelled a Jew they saw among the bystanders, Simon of Cyrene, to carry the burden for him.

When they reached Calvary Jesus was offered drugged wine to drink, but he refused it. After the soldiers had taken off his clothes, they put the crossbeam on the ground and, laying Jesus on it with outstretched arms, they drove nails through his hands into the wood. Then they lifted the crossbeam, with Jesus nailed to it, and bound it with ropes to the upright, high enough so that Jesus' feet would not reach the ground. Then they nailed Jesus' feet to the upright and, sitting down, they threw dice to decide how Jesus' clothes would be divided among them, and settled themselves to stay there until Jesus died. No wonder that Cicero, who lived in Rome before Jesus was born, called crucifixion "the most cruel and the most hideous of tortures"!

Fastened to the upright beam of the cross just above Jesus' head was an inscription, "The King of the Jews."

There Jesus hung from nine o'clock in the morning until three o'clock in the afternoon, when he died. We know only a little of what happened during those six dreadful hours. The disciples, so far as we know, were not present at the crucifixion, but some faithful women who had come with him from Galilee were there. Mark names three of them and says that there were more. They stood by Jesus to the end. But it was his enemies who gathered closest to the cross. They mocked and jeered him, we are told in the Gospels. They wagged their heads at him in scorn and challenged him to show that he really was the Messiah by coming down from the cross. "He saved others," they cried in derision, "let him save himself, if this is the Christ of God."

Two robbers were crucified with Jesus, one on either side of him. Luke says that one of the bandits abused Jesus, while the other stood up for him, saying that they were being punished justly but that Jesus had done nothing wrong. As to what Jesus himself said while he was on the cross, Mark and Matthew recall only one utterance of his. Just as death drew near,

They mocked him, crying, "Hail, King of the Jews."

they say, Jesus cried out, in the words of the twenty-second Psalm, "My God, my God, why hast Thou forsaken me?" Luke, however, recalls other things he said, especially his prayer for his enemies, "Father, forgive them; for they know not what they do," and his final cry of faith and trust, "Father, into Thy hands I commit my spirit."

So death came at last and delivered Jesus from his agony. The Sanhedrin wanted him buried before sunset, when the Sabbath began; so one of its members, Joseph of Arimathaea, asked Pilate for the body, and hurriedly laid it away in a tomb cut from the solid rock, with a stone rolled over the entrance.

That looked like the end of Jesus—his utter and complete defeat. One wonders what Caiaphas or Pilate would have said that Friday night, or what the devoted women who watched the crucifixion would have thought, if they had been told that sometime millions of people around the world would be singing about that cruel tragedy,

> *"In the cross of Christ I glory,*
> *Towering o'er the wrecks of time."*

It is not difficult to picture to ourselves the heartbreaking dismay of the disciples when Jesus was crucified. Despite all that he had foretold about his coming death, they never had imagined anything so savagely cruel befalling God's Messiah. They must have been utterly discouraged. We do not know just where the eleven disciples were when Jesus died on Calvary. Some think they had fled north to Galilee;

Death delivered Jesus from his agony.

others think they stayed in Jerusalem. Wherever they were, however, they certainly were a frightened group, their faith broken and their hopes crushed.

Yet, a few days afterward, they were on fire with such joy and enthusiasm as they had never known before. They were thinking and speaking in terms not of defeat but of victory. The cross which had seemed such a desperate tragedy became in their eyes a glorious triumph. Something amazing must have happened to lift them out of their dismay into such exalted confidence and hope that they went out to found the Christian church and to proclaim the good news to the ends of the earth. The New Testament leaves us in no doubt concerning what caused this astonishing transformation. The disciples became absolutely convinced that Jesus was not dead, that they had seen him alive and victorious, and that he would always be with them, an abiding Presence in their hearts and in the world.

The earliest written report which we have concerning Christ's resurrection is contained in the Apostle Paul's first letter to the church in Corinth. There Paul lists six appearances of the risen Jesus: to Peter, to the disciples, to "more than five hundred brethren at one time," to James, to all the apostles, and last of all to Paul himself in the vision on the Damascus road. Paul wrote this letter over thirty years after Jesus' death, and about fifteen years before the earliest Gospel was written by Mark.

The Gospels all end with stories of the way Jesus appeared to his friends and followers. Those downhearted men were filled with astonishment and disbelief when first they heard the news of Jesus' resurrection. When Mary Magdalene and her companions told the disciples about the empty tomb Mark says that "they would not believe it," and Luke says that "these words seemed to them an idle tale, and they did not believe them." But in the end, both in Jerusalem and later in Galilee, the appearances of Jesus were so convincing that doubt was conquered, and they were lifted from dismay to victory. Jesus was alive—they were certain about that.

When you grow older and read the learned books which Christian scholars have written about the resur-

rection of Jesus from the dead, you will see how widely
different are the views they hold. Some take literally
the stories about the resurrection of Jesus' body.
Others think that Jesus' appearances were not physical
but spiritual, like Paul's vision of Christ on the Damascus road, which changed him from a persecutor
of the church into a devoted Christian apostle. As the
years pass, you may make up your minds about such
disputed matters, but the central fact does not depend
on which views of such matters you accept. The central fact is the certainty of those disciples that Jesus
was alive, that they had seen him, that he was victor
over death and the grave.

That assured faith sent them out more confident
than they had ever been that Jesus was the Christ and
that, far from being defeated, the future belonged to
him and would see him triumph. Moreover, while no
longer physically with them, he was to them hence-
forth a living Presence, so that Paul could say, "It is
no longer I who live, but Christ who lives in me."
Something tremendous must have happened to change
those dismayed disciples, appalled at their Master's

death, into the builders of the Christian church, and we celebrate it still every Easter.

> *"Christ the Lord is risen today,*
> *Alleluia!"*

INDEX

Index

Boyhood (*Continued*)
  and Mary, 5-6, 13
  out-of-doors for, 14-17
  presentation to congregation, 19
  taught carpentry, 9
Buddhism, and miracles, 89

Caesar, 3
Caesarea Philippi, 106
Caiaphas, 161-163
Calvary, 170, 174, 176
Capernaum, 47-54, 111
Challenge to Jerusalem, 139-158
Children, 8-10
  education, 17-19
Christian Church, founding of, 89, 96, 124, 131, 176, 179
Christmas stories, 45
Chuza's wife, Joanna, 103
Cicero, 171
"City of David," 11
Crucifixion, 168-173
  prayer on cross, 127
  and Sadducees, 27

David, 11, 75
Disciples, 124
  See also Apostles
  ages of, 122
  ate Passover together, 152-154
  at Caesarea Philippi, 106
  and Calvary, 174, 176
  call to self-sacrifice, 107, 112
  failures to understand, 121
  faith shared with, 130-131

feeding five thousand people, 91
  and founding of Christian Church, 82, 96, 124, 176, 179
  and Gospel, 21, 38-41, 131
  four fishermen, 47-49, 57, 120
  in Gethsemane, 154-157, 164, 174, 176
  and idea of Messiah, 94-96, 106, 110, 112
  and racial prejudice, 131-134
  seventy, on mission, 124
  teaching of, 9-10
    last days in Jerusalem, 148-150
    lessons for, 13-14
    and training for victory, 119-135
  twelve, 57, 120

Easter, 179
Education of Jesus, 12-13, 17-21
Eleazar, 55-56
Elijah, 103, 106, 113
Elisha, 87-88
Esdraelon, 4, 15, 19

Family of Jesus, 8, 11-14, 19-20, 22, 81-82
Feast of Passover, 19, 139, 153
Followers, 81-96
  in Galilee, 54-58, 82, 99
  in Idumea, 83
  in Jordan, 83
  and physical welfare, 38
  seventy, 120
  speaking in their homes, 57

Index

Index

Index

Mary, 5-6, 12-13, 21, 46, 82
Mary Magdalene, 130, 177
Matthew, Apostle, 58-59
  quotes from, 12
    on Jesus, 106-107, 128, 148, 172-173
    on Peter, 106-107
    on Pilate's decision, 168
Messiah, 30-31
  popular ideas of, 28-29, 36
    and Christ's, of suffering, 106-107, 110, 112
  quote from Isaiah, 108-109
  Roman version, 163-164
  term defined, 28
  Zechariah's description, 139-140
Ministry of Jesus, 29, 45-48, 82, 99, 114
Miracles, 86-94, 95
Mohammedanism, 89
Moneylenders, 142-146
Moses, 105, 113
Mount Hermon, 4, 15
Mount of Olives, 154

New Testament, 77, 176
Nicodemus, 68

Old Testament, 50, 76-77, 87-88

Palestine, 4, 12, 25-26, 47-53
Palm Sunday, 83, 140
Parables and Sayings, 75, 85, 96, 123-124, 132, 148
Passover, 19, 139, 152-154
Paul, Apostle
  letters, 77

  first to church in Corinth, 176
  and resurrection, 177-178
Persians, 64
Peter, Apostle, 47, 49, 57-58
  boldness in courtroom, 120-121
  faith and belief, 106, 155, 164-165
  and lessons in forgiveness, 126-127
  and resurrection, 177
  at Transfiguration, 113
Pharisees, and Jesus, 59, 63-68, 75-77, 94, 103, 105, 128, 135, 148
  and "Messiah," 28, 77
  and our Puritans, 66-67
  and Paul, 77
Pharisees
  rules and regulations, 65-75, 83-84
Pilate, Pontius, 26-27, 151, 162, 166-170
Plain of Esdraelon, 4, 15, 19
Prodigal Son, 128, 130
Public ministry, 29, 45-58, 82, 99, 114
Puritans, 66-67

Racial prejudice, 131-134
Resurrection, 120, 176-178
Romans, 25-26, 27, 64, 77

Sadducees, 27-28, 75-76, 81, 94
Salome, 102
Samaria, 4, 111
Samaritans, 122, 132
Sanhedrin, 161, 162-164

Index